A John Hope Franklin Cente

anet **Books**

lited by Dilip Gaonkar, Jane Kramer,

Lee, and Michael Warner

lanet Books is a series designed by writers in and
he academy — writers working on what could be
rratives of public culture — to explore questions that
concern us all. It is an attempt to open scholarly
e on contemporary public culture, both local and
onal, and to illuminate that discourse with the kinds
ive that will challenge sophisticated readers, make
nk, and especially make them question. It is, most
tly, an experiment in strategies of discourse, com-
portage and critical reflection on unfolding issues
ts — one, we hope, that will provide a running narra-
r societies at this moment. Public Planet Books is
e Public Works publication project of the Center for
ural Studies, which also includes the journal *Public*
nd the Public Worlds book series.

public planet books

Fear of Small Numbers ▬▬▬▬▬

Fear of Small Numbers

An Essay on the Geography of Anger

Arjun Appadurai

DUKE UNIVERSITY PRESS *Durham and London 2006*

© 2006 Duke University Press

All rights reserved

Printed in the United States of

America on acid-free paper ♾

Typeset in Bodoni Book

by Tseng Information Systems.

Library of Congress Cataloging-

in-Publication Data appear on

the last printed page of this book.

3rd printing, 2006

An earlier version of chapter 4

appeared as "The New Logics of

Violence," *Seminar* 503 (2001).

Contents

Preface

This long essay is the second installment in a long-term project that began in 1989. The first phase of that project was an effort to examine the cultural dynamics of the then emerging world of globalization and resulted in a book entitled *Modernity at Large: Cultural Dimensions of Globalization* (1996). That study raised some analytical and ethical doubts about the future of the nation-state and sought to examine the ways in which the twin forces of media and migration had created new resources for the work of the imagination as a social practice. In addition to suggesting some patterns in the way that culture, media, and transitional diasporas were mutually structuring forces in a world of disjunctures, *Modernity at Large* proposed that the production of lived communities, localities, had become further complicated in the context of globalization.

The 1996 book provoked much debate both within and beyond anthropology. Some critics saw the book as presenting too rosy a picture of the globalization of the early 1990s and as being insufficiently attentive to the darker sides of globalization, such as violence, exclusion, and growing inequality. In part as a consequence of these questions, and in part driven by my own longer-term interests, I began to do research on collective violence against Muslims in my home city (Bombay, now called Mumbai), where there had been intense riots between Hindus and Muslims in January 1992 and later in 1993. These episodes of group violence were part of a national wave of attacks on Muslims shrines, homes, and populations across India in the wake of the destruction of the Babri Masjid in Ayodhya in December 1992. This work on Hindu-Muslim violence in Mumbai in the 1990s was part of a broader comparative project on large-scale ethnocidal violence in the world after 1989, notably in Rwanda and Central Europe but also in India and elsewhere. The results of these inquiries in the decade since 1995 are partly reflected here, as well as in some essays published in the intervening decade, parts of which have been drawn upon in this book.

This research into some of the harshest results of globalization—and this book is intended to argue these connections—also brought me, mostly by accident, into contact with an entirely new phenomenon, a phenomenon from which we can all draw hope about the future of globalization. In Mumbai, while looking at the violence against Muslims in this historically mostly liberal and cosmopolitan city, my dear friend Sundar Burra introduced me to a remarkable group of activists, to which he belonged, who gave me access to their work among the poorest of the urban poor in Mumbai. They also introduced me to what was in 1996 still a little studied phenomenon—the phenomenon of grassroots globalization, globalization from below, the worldwide effort of activist nongovernmental organizations and movements to seize and shape the global agenda on such matters as human rights, gender, poverty, environment, and disease. This remarkable encounter in Mumbai led me to embark on a parallel research project on grassroots globalization, whose preliminary results I allude to in the last pages of this book. The full story of these Mumbai housing activists and the implications for the politics of hope are the subject of a study (with the tentative title *The Capacity to Aspire*) that is now in the final stages of preparation.

Thus the book you have begun to read is a transition and a pause in a long-term project—both intellectual and personal—to seek ways to make globalization work for those who need it most and enjoy it least, the poor, the dispossessed, the weak, and the marginal populations of our world. It is a transition because all talk of hope is idle unless it is pulled out of the jaws of the brutality which globalization has also produced. And until we understand how globalization can produce new forms of hatred, ethnocide, and ideocide, we will not know where to seek the resources for hope about globalization and the globalization of hope. So I ask the reader to bear with me on this phase of an investigation that is not yet complete.

As always, I have many debts to friends and colleagues. A decade is a long time, and I have been the beneficiary of generosity in many countries and continents during this time. The full list of individuals and audiences that helped me shape the chapters of this book would be too long to be meaningful. So I must run the risk of unfairness and pick out just a few names who have helped in various ways throughout the (all too slow) evolution of this study. In alphabetical order, they are Jockin Arputham, Brian Axel, Sundar Burra, Dipesh Chakrabarty, Jean Comaroff, John Comaroff, Neera Chandoke, Veena Das, Celine D'Cruz, Faisal Devji, Dilip Gaonkar, Peter Geschiere, Rashid Khalidi, David Laitin, Benjamin Lee, Claudio Lomnitz, Achille Mbembe, Uday Mehta, Sheela Patel, Vyjayanthi Rao, Kumkum Sangaree, Charles Taylor, Peter van der Veer and Ken Wissoker. Two anonymous readers for Duke University Press asked searching questions that have affected the final version substantially.

Some institutional thanks are also in order. The Open Society Institute in New York gave me an Individual Fellowship in 1997–98 to work on this subject. The University of Chicago gave me sabbatical leave and other support to complete this book. Yale University and the University of Chicago offered me teaching opportunities and student interlocutors who honed my arguments. The Department of Political Science at the University of Delhi appointed me as a visiting professor and invited me to offer the Teen Murti series of lectures in February 2002, which form the basis of chapters 2, 5, and 6. The New School reminded me, most recently, of the value of dissent and debate for global democratic practice. I am grateful to each of these institutions.

There are some debts closer to home. Ajay Gandhi and Nikhil Anand at Yale University were close readers and thoughtful critics of the entire text. Zack Fine and Leilah Vevaina at the New School struggled with an ever-changing manuscript to bring it to this stage. Last but not least, my wife, Carol A. Breckenridge, hovered over this book. Without her encouragement and prodding, neither its soul nor its substance would have come to light.

Bethany, Connecticut
August 2005

xiii

1 From Ethnocide to Ideocide

This study is concerned with large-scale, culturally motivated violence in our times. Its chapters, whose arguments are previewed here, were drafted between 1998 and 2004. Thus, their principal arguments were developed in the shadow of two major kinds of violence. The first kind, which we saw in Eastern Europe, Rwanda, and India in the early 1990s, showed that the world after 1989 was not going to be entirely progressive and that globalization could expose severe pathologies in the sacred ideologies of nationhood. The second kind, officially globalized under the rubric of the "war on terror," may be marked by the cataclysmic attacks on the World Trade Center in New York and the Pentagon in Virginia on September 11, 2001. This latter event bracketed the 1990s as a decade of superviolence, a decade characterized by a steady growth in civil and civic warfare in many societies as a feature of everyday life. We now live in a world, articulated differently by states and by media in different national and regional contexts, in which fear often appears to be the source and ground for intensive campaigns of group violence, ranging from riots to extended pogroms.

In the 1940s and for some time after, many scholars began to assume that extreme forms of collective violence, especially those combining large-scale killing with various forms of planned degradation of the human body and human dignity, were direct by-products of totalitarianism, notably of fascism, and were discernable in Mao's China, in Stalin's Soviet Union, and in smaller totalitarian societies. Alas, the 1990s have left no doubt that liberal-democratic societies, as well as a variety of mixed state forms, are susceptible to capture by majoritarian forces and large-scale ethnocidal violence.

2   So we are forced to ask and answer the question about why the 1990s, the period of what we may now call "high globalization," should also be the period of large-scale violence in a wide range of societies and political regimes? In referring to high globalization (with more than a gesture to high modernism), I flag a set of utopian possibilities and projects that swept many countries, states, and public spheres after the end of the Cold War. These possibilities were captured in a series of intertwined doctrines about open markets and free trade, about the spread of democratic institutions and liberal constitutions, and about the powerful possibilities of the Internet (and related cyber technologies) to mitigate inequality both within and across societies and to increase freedom, transparency, and good governance in even the poorest and most isolated countries. Today, only the most fundamentalist supporters of unfettered economic globalization assume that the domino effects of free trade and high degrees of cross-national market integration and capital flow are always positive.

Thus, this work is one more attempt to address the following question: why should a decade dominated by a global endorsement of open markets, free flow of finance capital, and liberal ideas of constitutional rule, good governance, and active expansion of human rights have produced a plethora of examples of ethnic cleansing on one hand and extreme forms of political violence against civilian populations (a fair definition of terrorism as a tactic) on the other? In the course of what follows, I shall occasionally take issue with some prominent efforts to tackle this question. Here, I confine myself to stating, in simple terms, the ingredients of a different sort of answer, an answer rooted in a preoccupation with the cultural dimensions of globalization. Some critics saw my earlier effort to characterize the (then) emerging world of globalization (1996) as perhaps a bit too harsh in its criticisms of the modern nation-state and as naively cheerful about the benefits of global flows. This essay addresses the darker sides of globalization directly.

3

To arrive at a better understanding of what globalization may have to do with ethnic cleansing and with terror I propose a series of interlocking ideas. The first step is to recognize that there is a fundamental, and dangerous, idea behind the very idea of the modern nation-state, the idea of a "national ethnos." No modern nation, however benign its political system and however eloquent its public voices may be about the virtues of tolerance, multiculturalism, and inclusion, is free of the idea that its national sovereignty is built on some sort of ethnic genius. We have just seen this point of view expressed with shocking civility by Samuel Huntington (2004), in an open call to alarm about the way in which Hispanic people in the United States are threatening to secede from the American way, seen as a narrow Euro-Protestant cultural doctrine. So much for the idea that ethnonationalist positions are confined to dark Baltic states, raving African demagogues, or fringe Nazis in England and northern Europe.

It has been widely noted that the idea of a singular national ethnos, far from being a natural outgrowth of this or that soil, has been produced and naturalized at great cost, through rhetorics of war and sacrifice, through punishing disciplines of educational and linguistic uniformity, and through the subordination of myriad local and regional traditions to produce Indians or Frenchmen or Britons or Indonesians (Anderson 1991; Balibar 1990; Scott 1998; Weber 1976). It has also been observed by some of our great political theorists, notably Hannah Arendt (1968), that the idea of a national peoplehood is the Achilles' heel of modern liberal societies. In the argument here, I draw on the ideas of Mary Douglas and other anthropologists, to suggest that the road from national genius to a totalized cosmology of the sacred nation, and further to ethnic purity and cleansing, is relatively direct. There are those that argue that this is only a risk in those modern polities that have mistakenly put blood at the center of their national ideology, but blood and nationalism appear to be in a much fuller and wider embrace in the world as a whole. All nations, under some conditions, demand whole-blood transfusions, usually requiring some part of their blood to be extruded.

This inherent ethnicist tendency in all ideologies of nationalism does not explain why only some national polities become the scenes of large-scale violence, civil war, or ethnic cleansing. Here we need recourse to a second idea, involving the place of social uncertainty in social life. In an earlier essay entitled "Dead Certainty" (1998b), I develop a detailed argument about the ways in which social uncertainty can drive projects of ethnic cleansing that are both vivisectionist and verificationist in their procedures. That is, they seek uncertainty by dismembering the suspect body, the body under suspicion. This species of uncertainty is intimately connected to the reality that today's ethnic groups number in the hundreds of thousands and that their movements, mixtures, cultural styles, and media representations create profound doubts about who exactly are among the "we" and who are among the "they."

The speed and intensity with which both material and ideological elements now circulate across national boundaries have created a new order of uncertainty in social life. Whatever may characterize this new kind of uncertainty, it does not easily fit the dominant, Weberian prophecy about modernity in which earlier, intimate social forms would dissolve, to be replaced by highly regimented bureaucratic-legal orders governed by the growth of procedure and predictability. The forms of such uncertainty are certainly various. One kind of uncertainty is a direct reflection of census concerns: how many persons of this or that sort really exist in a given territory? Or, in the context of rapid migration or refugee movement, how many of "them" are there now among us? Another kind of uncertainty is about what some of these mega identities really mean: for example, what are the normative characteristics of what the constitution defines as a member of an OBC (Other Backward Caste) in India? A further uncertainty is about whether a particular person really is what he or she claims or appears to be or has historically been. Finally, these various forms of uncertainty create intolerable anxiety about the relationship of many individuals to state-provided goods—ranging from housing and health to safety and sanitation—since these entitlements are frequently directly tied to who "you" are and thus to who "they" are. Each kind of uncertainty gains increasing force whenever there are large-scale movements of persons (for whatever reason), when new rewards or risks attach to large-scale ethnic identities, or when existing networks of social knowledge are eroded by rumor, terror, or social movement. Where one or more of these forms of social uncertainty come into play, violence can create a macabre form of certainty and can become a brutal technique (or folk discovery-procedure) about "them" and, therefore, about "us." This volatile relationship between certainty and uncertainty might make special sense in the era of globalization.

In this context, in myriad ways, some essential principles and procedures of the modern nation-state—the idea of a sovereign and stable territory, the idea of a containable and countable population, the idea of a reliable census, and the idea of stable and transparent categories—have come unglued in the era of globalization, for reasons explored in the chapters that follow. Above all, the certainty that distinctive and singular peoples grow out of and control well-defined national territories has been decisively unsettled by the global fluidity of wealth, arms, peoples, and images that I described in *Modernity at Large* (1996).

In simpler words, where the lines between us and them may have always, in human history, been blurred at the boundaries and unclear across large spaces and big numbers, globalization exacerbates these uncertainties and produces new incentives for cultural purification as more nations lose the illusion of national economic sovereignty or well-being. This observation also reminds us that large-scale violence is not simply the product of antagonistic identities but that violence itself is one of the ways in which the illusion of fixed and charged identities is produced, partly to allay the uncertainties about identity that global flows invariably produce. In this regard, Islamic fundamentalism, Christian fundamentalism, and many other local and regional forms of cultural fundamentalism may be seen as a part of an emerging repertoire of efforts to produce previously unrequired levels of certainty about social identity, values, survival, and dignity. Violence, especially extreme and spectacular violence, is a mode of producing such certainty by mobilizing what I have elsewhere called "full attachment" (1998a), especially when the forces of social uncertainty are allied to other fears about growing inequality, loss of national sovereignty, or threats to local security and livelihood. In this sense, one of the repeat motifs of my own arguments here is that, to use Philip Gourevitch's brutal aphorism about Rwanda, "genocide, after all, is an exercise in community-building" (1998: 95).

The social productivity of violence does not in itself account for the special ways in which violence against groups defined as minorities seems to have taken on a new life in the 1990s, from the United States to Indonesia and from Norway to Nigeria. One could argue that the still contested European Union is in many ways the most enlightened political formation in the postnational world. Yet, there are two Europes in evidence today: the world of inclusion and multiculturalism in one set of European societies and the anxious xenophobia of what we may call Pim Fortuyn's Europe (Austria, Romania, Holland, France). To account for why otherwise inclusive, democratic, even secular national states spawn ideologies of majoritarianism and racialized nationalism, we need to probe more deeply into the heart of liberalism, as I do in chapter 4.

That analysis leads me to observe that the tip-over into ethnonationalism and even ethnocide in democratic polities has much to do with the strange inner reciprocity of the categories of "majority" and "minority" in liberal social thought, which produces what I call the *anxiety of incompleteness*. Numerical majorities can become predatory and ethnocidal with regard to *small numbers* precisely when some minorities (and their small numbers) remind these majorities of the small gap which lies between their condition as majorities and the horizon of an unsullied national whole, a pure and untainted national ethnos. This sense of incompleteness can drive majorities into paroxysms of violence against minorities, in conditions that I analyze in special detail with respect to Muslims in India throughout the book, especially in chapter 5.

Globalization, as a specific way in which states, markets, and ideas about trade and governance have come to be organized, exacerbates the conditions of large-scale violence because it produces a potential collision course between the logics of uncertainty and incompleteness, each of which has its own form and force. As a broad fact about the world of the 1990s, the forces of globalization produced conditions for an increase in large-scale social uncertainty and also in the friction of incompleteness, both of which emerged in the traffic between the categories of majority and minority. The anxiety of incompleteness (always latent in the project of complete national purity) and the sense of social uncertainty about large-scale ethnoracial categories can produce a runaway form of mutual stimulation, which is the road to genocide.

This approach to the growth in large-scale cultural violence in the 1990s — combining uncertainty and incompleteness — can also provide an angle (neither a model nor an explanation) on the problem of why such violence occurs in a relatively small number of cases, especially if the total universe is measured by the current number of independent nation-states. The argument presented here — which pivots on the relationship between globalization, uncertainty, and incompleteness — allows us a way to recognize when the anxiety of incompleteness and unacceptable levels of uncertainty combine in ways that spark large-scale ethnocidal mobilization. One might argue that the co-presence of high levels of both sentiments is a necessary condition of large-scale violence. But sufficiency, as is so often the case in the social sciences, is another matter. Sufficiency might be provided by a rogue state (Iraq and the Kurds), by a racist colonial structure (Rwanda), by a tragically ethnicized constitution-building process (Yugoslavia after Tito), or by criminal leaders driven by personal greed and illicit commodity networks (Liberia, Sudan). In India, which is a central example throughout this book, the condition of sufficiency appears to have to do with a special contingency that links a major political partition to a series of internal legal and cultural fault lines.

One more point needs to be made. The large-scale violence of the 1990s appears to be typically accompanied by a surplus of rage, an excess of hatred that produces untold forms of degradation and violation, both to the body and the being of the victim: maimed and tortured bodies, burned and raped persons, disemboweled women, hacked and amputated children, sexualized humiliation of every type. What are we to do with this surplus, which has frequently been enacted in public actions, often among friends and neighbors, and is no longer conducted in the covert ways in which the degradation of group warfare used to occur in the past? Considering the many elements that go into a possible answer, I suggest that this excess has something to do with the deformations that globalization has brought to the "narcissism of minor differences," a theme I address in chapter 4.

The core of that argument about the surplus of rage, the urge to degradation, is that the narcissism of minor differences is now vastly more dangerous than in the past because of the new economy of slippage and morphing which characterizes the relationship between majority and minority identities and powers. Since the two categories, owing to the pliability of censuses, constitutions, and changing ideologies of inclusion and equity, can plausibly change places, minor differences are no longer just valued tokens of an uncertain self and thus especially to be protected, as the original Freudian insight might suggest. In fact, minor differences can become the least acceptable ones, since they further lubricate the slippery two-way traffic between the two categories. The brutality, degradation, and dehumanization that have frequently accompanied the ethnicized violence of the past fifteen years are a sign of conditions in which the very line between minor and major differences has been made uncertain. In these circumstances, the rage and fear that incompleteness and uncertainty together produce can no longer be addressed by the mechanical extinction or extrusion of unwanted minorities. Minority is the symptom but difference itself is the underlying problem. Thus the elimination of difference itself (not just the hyper-attachment to *minor* differences) is the new hallmark of today's large-scale, *predatory narcissisms*. Since the elimination of difference project is fundamentally impossible in a world of blurred boundaries, mixed marriages, shared languages, and other deep connectivities, it is bound to produce an order of frustration that can begin to account for the systematic excess that we see in today's headlines. The psychodynamics and social psychology of this line of inquiry, a difficult subject well beyond my own expertise, require deeper exploration than presented in chapter 4.

These ideas about uncertainty, incompleteness, minorities, and the productivity of violence in the era of globalization may allow us to reposition the world of unilateral and perpetual war and long-distance democratization, unveiled by the United States in Afghanistan and Iraq after 9/11, and the world of long-distance terror, unleashed by Al-Qaeda and others against the West in the same period. Chapters 2, 5, and 6 were written in the immediate aftermath of 9/11 and were composed in Europe and India in the six months that followed the attacks on the World Trade Center and Pentagon. Some things have changed since then, but not others.

The new sorts of cellular political organization (represented by Al-Qaeda), the increasing reliance in asymmetric warfare of violence against civilian populations, the growth in the tactic of suicide bombing, and, most recently, the tactic of the broadcast beheading (of more or less casual participants in scenes of violent struggle) force us to ask yet a new set of questions. These concern the sources of global rage against the forces of the market, the special nature of recent anti-Americanism in many parts of the world, and the odd return of the body of the patriot, the martyr, and the sacrificial victim into the spaces of mass violence.

Let me conclude this overview by focusing on the most recent form of public and mass-mediated shock to enter the dramas of violence staged in the name of religion, nationality, freedom, and identity, namely the videotaped kidnappings of victims in Iraq and, in some instances, their beheading, as a media tool for exerting asymmetric pressure on various states, most recently including India, by groups associated with militant Islam. In some ways, we see a return here to the simplest form of religious violence, the sacrifice, about which René Girard (1977) has written eloquently. Starting with the videotaped beheading of Daniel Pearl in Pakistan soon after 9/11, the public sacrifice has grown into a more systematic tool of political expression. Those who are kidnapped and actually beheaded or under threat of being beheaded are not necessarily wealthy, powerful, or famous. They include, for example, a poor and desperate group of labor migrants to Iraq from India, Kuwait, and elsewhere. These poor migrants, themselves fodder in the traffic of globalization, signal a counterpoint to the impersonal death produced by the United States Air Force in Iraq or by Al-Qaeda in New York City, Nairobi, and Saudi Arabia over the past few years. Televised beheadings in Iraq stage a strong gesture to a more intimate and personal sacrifice by combining known and identifiable victims with a more gradual and deliberate ceremony of violent death, a more stately drama of the armed powers "behind the mask." These tragic victims are the involuntary counterparts of the suicide bombers of Palestine, Iraq, and Sri Lanka. In these cases, ideologies produced by various forms of desperation about asymmetry produce victims and martyrs as instruments of freedom. These singular bodies are a desperate effort to bring back a religious element to spaces of death and destruction that have become unimaginably abstract. They might also be viewed as moral responses, however shocking, to the tortured, leashed, humiliated, and photographed bodies of Muslim men in American custody in Iraq and Afghanistan.

2 The Civilization of Clashes

In the way we think about political peace and social order, certain items of conceptual furniture have long been in place. These include the following clichés: that the modern nation-state is the sole owner of large-scale decisions to conduct war and make enduring arrangements for peace; that social order in everyday life is a default state, assured by the sheer absence of war; and that there is a deep and natural distinction between the social disorder within societies and war across societies. Each of these verities stands shattered in the world after 9/11. Within the past few years, we have come to see that warfare has escaped the context of the nation-state and has exceeded the logics of any sort of realism. Likewise, we are faced with forms of ethnic conflict that verge on low-intensity warfare and have become the routine or default state of affairs in many societies; the old joke about outbreaks of peace is now a sobering social fact. Finally, the metastasis of what we call terrorism and the rapid-fire spread in the discourse of terrorism as a name for any variety of antistate activity has decisively blurred the lines between wars *of* the nation and wars *in* the nation.

The disturbance of these verities, of course, did not come unannounced even if it carried more than its share of the enigmas of arrival. Internal wars, by various counts, have outnumbered external wars for some decades now. Warfare in civilian zones, conducted with a view to eliminating the idea of war as a regulated activity between armed combatants, has been with us for some time. Mass murder of civilian populations, perhaps first made an official instrument by the Nazis, has been commonplace in the ethnic wars of the past few decades. And the spread of militias at every level of society, especially in societies marked by weak or dependent states, have unmoored the flag, the uniform, and the automatic rifle from the official nation-state in many world regions.

Yet, something did happen on 9/11 which brought these gradual developments to a head and forced us to rethink some of our cherished assumptions about war, peace, and state-sponsored security. The attack on the Twin Towers has been analyzed more closely than James Joyce's *Ulysses* and with as much variation in opinion. But few would deny that in attacking the belly of the beast, in sneaking into the heart of lightness and bringing down the Buddhas of Wall Street, a new kind of war was declared. Its newness was not in its technological asymmetry, though it was striking in that regard. Nor was its newness in its audacious effort to terrorize an entire megacity and produce chaos in the high-speed machinery of global capital. And nor was it to be found in the effort to produce terror through a form of high-tech meltdown.

Its newness was its effort to inaugurate a war defined only by an enemy, the enemy being the United States. Being an unsigned act of war, a kind of Dadaist nightmare, a monstrous form of revenge for all the Hollywood scenarios of urban terror, Arab bombers, attacks from alien forces, and the like, 9/11 moved the idea of the authorless war to a new level of seriousness.

Nor was it that this was a war undertaken by an unnamed force. It was war undertaken by a new type of agency, an agency neither interested in establishing a state nor in opposing any particular state, nor in the relations between states at all. This was a war against America, but it was also a war against the idea that states are the only game in town. The 9/11 attacks were a massive act of social punishment, a kind of massive public execution, a death by fire, stone, and rubble intended to punish America for its moral travesties around the world, in particular in the Islamic world.

It is this moral, punitive, and pedagogical quality to the attacks of 9/11 that have led some observers to turn to Samuel Huntington's famous model of the clash of civilizations (1993), although many more have questioned the relevance of the model. But before we take issue with it, let us note what appeal it holds after 9/11. It points to a new sort of moral outrage at work in the world today, a new willingness to conduct extreme acts of war in the name of specific ideas of moral purity and social rectitude, and it is of course foolish to deny that there is some powerful link between social forces in the Islamic world and the events of 9/11.

There are many nontrivial reasons to look beyond the Huntington model, and I take them up again in chapter 6. For now, let me make only a few observations. The Islamic world is full of its own internal debates. Not least among these debates is the question of which Islamic states are seen as just states by their own people and which are not. And many Islamic states are treated as illegitimate by various coalitions which want to attack non-Islamic ones, notably the United States and Great Britain. To the extent that Al-Qaeda was mainly responsible for the attacks of 9/11 and that Osama bin Laden was the mastermind behind this network, it also seems clear that he represents a highly specific variety of moral and eschatological dissent within the Islamic world and within the Arab, Saudi, and Sunni worlds. This may be a war in the name of Islam, but its authority derives from much more idiosyncratic sources within the Islamic world.

I will return to my reasons for preferring to think of ourselves as being in a worldwide civilization of clashes rather than in a clash of civilizations later, but I want now to set the stage by looking at the American reaction to the events of 9/11.

The American Reaction

In a curious way, it was not until the U.S. government reacted, after about a week of recovery from the sheer shock of the attacks, that we could begin to see something of the morphology of the new war and the sort of clash it represented. Much has been written about the groping for appropriate words by the U.S. media and within state organs to describe the unseen and unknown enemy. We can look back now and praise the initial effort to avoid explicitly racist language, to avoid inflaming anti-Arab sentiments, to resist the temptation to name the entire Islamic world as the enemy. Indeed, Condoleezza Rice, then the National Security Advisor, early on declared that this was *not* a clash of civilizations (thus clearly repudiating Huntington). George Bush and other leading members of his administration joined the desperate struggle to name the enemy, and slowly the naming process took shape. Al-Qaeda, Afghanistan, and Osama bin Laden emerged within two weeks after 9/11 as the proper names with which to tell the unfolding story of the outrage that had been perpetrated upon the American people and to shape the justification of the powerful military reaction that was unleashed shortly thereafter.

This is not the place for an analysis of the extraordinary air war that was unleashed by the United States and Great Britain against Afghanistan, the Taliban, and the core leadership of the Al-Qaeda network. Much has been said about the bizarre humanitarianism of air-dropping food packages with bombs. Much too has been said about the irony of taking a country that the Taliban had reduced to rubble and turning it into dust. And about the intense terror that was produced in the devastated civilian populations of Afghanistan that had already been reduced to psychological wrecks by the Taliban. And, on the world stage, it has rightly been noted that the counterattack on Afghanistan allowed a sleepy war machine in the United States to come awake, allowed a barely elected leader in his first term in office to assume the mantle of savior of the civilized world, and let various characters replay the moral dramas of Suez, the Cold War, and the Gulf War, suitably telescoped into one gigantic drama of Gulliver enraged. The world was once more turned into a list of supporters and detractors, ayes and nays, supporters and opponents of what became the names of an ominous global enemy: terror, terrorism, terrorists.

The war against Afghanistan, still not quite over, was what we may call a *diagnostic* war, or even a forensic war. It was a war calculated to make discoveries. The most important diagnosis that the war sought to make was about who exactly the enemy was: What was Al-Qaeda? Who was Osama bin Laden? Who really were the Taliban? This was also a diagnostic war in another sense. It sought to identify the supporters of the United States and the United Kingdom; forced Europe and Japan to declare their loyalties; and made many fence-sitters fall on the side of the United States, whatever their reservations. This was a plebiscite called by the mighty U.S. war machine and abstentions were not permitted. Many of these features characterized the subsequent war on Iraq, though in the latter case the precipitating forensic question was about "weapons of mass destruction."

And because the enemy was named as a global terrorist network, itself linked by shadowy mechanisms to nameless other such networks with tentacles throughout the world, many states were able to identify with such naming of their own dissidents, antistate activists, and violent minorities. This was a name with a powerful global constituency. And most states recognized that this was a name with infinite possibilities for local manipulation. India was no exception.

But the main reason for this overwhelming show of support for the United States from governments throughout the world is that they recognized that the war unleashed on 9/11 was above all a war between two kinds of systems, both global in scope. The first may be described as *vertebrate*, the second as *cellular*. Modern nation-states recognize their common belonging to the vertebrate world and, like the last dinosaurs, see that they are in a desperate struggle for survival as a global formation.

Cellular Versus Vertebrate Systems

To understand the distinction between vertebrate and cellular world systems, we need to take a step back and reflect on the processes that we have come to designate with the word globalization. Although many debates surround the extent to which globalization has eroded the contours of the system of nation-states, no serious analyst of the global economy over the past three decades would deny that whatever may have been the initial fictions and contradictions of the nation-state, these have been brought into sharper view through the deeper integration of world markets and the extensive spread of ideologies of marketization worldwide, especially after 1989. Nor has this simply been a matter of balance of trade in relation to GDP. It is an institutional matter, which many scholars have shown to involve deep changes in the character of national institutions, such as central banks, which in many societies in effect make global policies within national settings. Whole bodies of cross-border law, accountancy, and information technology protocols have emerged, many not known or used beyond specialized technocratic elites, to govern complex forms of global economic traffic.

The idea of a national economy, always leaky at best (and no older than the German geographer Friedrich List), now looks most often collaborative and facilitative rather than autonomous or self-defined. Only the world's most powerful economies look national in any important respect and the biggest one of all, the United States economy, is nothing if it is not global. In Europe, there is widespread agreement that the largest justification for the European Union is the inescapable fact that Europe has to play the global game, or risk everything. The Japanese, not fully set up to go global in the new order of things, find themselves overnight a sedated economy, immune even to various macroeconomic electric shocks.

There is less agreement about the emergent politics and culture of this hyperglobalized world. But debates are afoot among various thinkers about the crisis of the nation-state, about the future of sovereignty, about the viability of states that are not part of strong regional coalitions. These debates, which have their counterparts in political speeches and mass movements throughout the world, often take the form of new panics about foreign goods or about foreign languages, foreign migrants, or foreign investments. Many states find themselves caught between the need to perform dramas of national sovereignty and simultaneous feats of openness calculated to invite the blessings of Western capital and the multilaterals.

The virtually complete loss of even the fiction of a national economy, which had some evidence for its existence in the eras of strong socialist states and central planning, now leaves the cultural field as the main one in which fantasies of purity, authenticity, borders, and security can be enacted. It is no surprise that throughout the developing world, the death or implosion of powerful national economies (through the growth in transient forms of foreign investment, the increase in transnational economic forms and processes, and the growth of offshore economic empires that escape all forms of national accounting) has been accompanied by the rise of various new fundamentalisms, majoritarianisms, and indigenisms, frequently with a marked ethnocidal edge. The nation-state has been steadily reduced to the fiction of its ethnos as the last cultural resource over which it may exercise full dominion.

And, of course, there is another side to the current dynamic of globalization, one noted by a wide range of observers. This is the growing production of greater inequality between nations, classes, and regions. This increase in inequality, irrespective of the expert debates about its precise links to open markets and high-velocity global capital flows, is seen at the popular level in many countries as a direct product of the unfettered force of global capitalism and its unquestioned national driver, the United States. It is doubtless this apparent link between imploding national economies, runaway financial capital, and the role of the United States as the main driver of the ideologies of business, market, and profit that has created a new sort of emotional Cold War between those who identify with the losers in the new game and those who identify with the small group of winners, notably the United States. The widely remarked sense that some sort of justice had been visited upon the United States even among those who abhorred the brutality of 9/11 is no doubt anchored in moral outrage driven by the logic of economic exclusion. There is more to the story of the growth in the global hatred of the United States, and I return to that topic in chapter 6.

What is noteworthy about the new flows of money, weapons, information, people, and ideologies across national boundaries is that they have produced forms of solidarity that exist on the same *political* plane as those that were traditionally monopolized by the nation-state. Thus, diasporic communities of many kinds command primary loyalties among populations that may also exist within various national boundaries. Debates on key issues of war, peace, identity, and progress rage among cyber communities that function across national lines and represent various kinds of solidarity, some cultural, some professional, some situational or opportunistic. Virulent nationalisms also thrive in the context of cyberspace, but they nevertheless complicate the solidity of the ties between space, place, and identity. There is really a community called eelam.com (Jeganathan 1998), which includes Tamils fleeing violence in Sri Lanka since the 1970s. Collective imaginings and imagined collectivities, in the era of cyber technologies, are no longer just two sides of the same coin. Rather, they frequently test and contest one another.

Images of the network have been invoked forcefully to capture the emergent social and political forms of this interconnected, technology-driven world, notably by Manuel Castells

(1996) but also by many corporate gurus, futurologists, and others. And the world is clearly now linked up by multiple circuits along which money, news, people, and ideas flow, meet, converge, and disperse again. And yet the image of the network seems too general for the reality it seeks to capture.

The idea of a *cellular* world seems slightly more precise. The contrast, derived from biology, contrasts cellular with vertebral forms and like all analogies, it is not intended to be complete or perfect. The modern system of nation-states is the most marked case of a *vertebrate* structure, for though nations thrive on their stories of difference and singularity, the system of nation-states works only because of its underlying assumption of an international order, guaranteed by a variety of norms, not least the norms of war itself. Today this vertebrate order is symbolized not just by the United Nations but by the large and growing body of protocols, institutions, treaties, and agreements that seek to ensure that all nations operate on symmetrical principles in relation to their conduct with one another, whatever their hierarchies in power or wealth. The system of nation-states has relied from the start on a system of semiotic recognition and communication, composed of such simple items as flags, stamps, and airlines and by much more complex systems such as those of consulates, ambassadors, and other mutual forms of recognition. Such vertebrate systems, of which the system of nation-states may be the largest and most extensive in scale, are not necessarily centralized or hierarchical. But they are fundamentally premised on a finite set of coordinated, regulative norms and signals. It is not difficult to see why the Treaty of Westphalia and the writings of Kant on moral reciprocity and symmetry came into being so close in time and space.

The global capitalist system does not fit clearly into the contrast between vertebrate and cellular systems. On the one hand, it is clearly a vertebrate system, relying as it does on a vast nervous system of communications, transport, long-distant credit, and coordinated fiscal transactions. This coordinated feature has always been part of the story of industrial capitalism, which at the very minimum required some reliable systems for credit and monetary exchange. Modern capitalism is also vertebrate in the sense that it requires the widespread applicability of certain protocols of law, accounting, policing, taxation, and security, for which it has typically relied on the arrangements between sovereign states, guaranteed by various agreements and treaties. In this sense the vertebrate structures of the system of nation-states and that of modern industrial capital have overlapping structures and an obviously interconnected history. This common structure was never free of tensions and contradictions, of course, but it is nevertheless visible in the global political economy as far back as the sixteenth and seventeenth centuries in maritime empires that came out of Western and Southern Europe.

But, on the other hand, as capitalism has evolved since the nineteenth century, as it has grown technically more sophisticated and portable, as its technologies have become more modular and mobile, and as its financial component has become increasingly free of direct relations with industry and manufacture, it has gradually begun to evolve certain crucial cellular features. These features have been increasingly visible in the era of capitalism that has variously been called "post-Fordist," "disorganized," "flexible," or "postindustrial." In this era, characterized by the shift from multinational corporations to transnational corporations, and now to global corporations, the high-velocity recombination of the factors of production has changed the geography of capital and made its movements and national profile hard to assess. These qualities, especially evident since the 1970s, have been reflected in many sorts of organizational slogans and models, all seeking to capture the mobile, recombinant, opportunistic, and de-nationalized workings of many global corporations. In the decades since the mid-1980s, these cellular features have been further accelerated by the linked growth of new information technologies and of the bewildering speed and scale of financial transactions that have made national financial markets subject to sudden and dramatic crises. This process has moved from Mexico to East Asia to Argentina, where a tremendously wealthy country was reduced to economic anarchy within a few weeks. Countries such as India have openly admitted that their relative immunity to such crises is at least partly a function of their weak integration into the global economy. Yet, this is a difficult game, as many countries in sub-Saharan Africa show us the disastrous implications of being too marginal to global market processes.

In various ways, the current state of global firms and the markets in which they operate display a split personality that resembles and relies on the vertebrate features of the nation-state system but also is the laboratory for new forms of cellularity, de-linkage, and local autonomy.

This double character of global capitalism in the era of the Internet is what allows us to understand better the cellular nature of the new "terrorist networks." Connected yet not vertically managed, coordinated yet remarkably independent, capable of replication without central messaging structures, hazy in their central organizational features yet crystal clear in their cellular strategies and effects, these organizations clearly rely on the crucial tools of money transfer, hidden organization, offshore havens, and nonofficial means of training and mobilization, which also characterize the workings of many levels of the capitalist world. Indeed, the grayer areas of the world of banking and finance are clearly complicit with the workings of the networks of international terror. The massive campaign to pursue and freeze the assets of these organizations through the vehicles of banking, taxation, and law, especially in the United States, is a clear testimony to the seriousness of this link. After all, there is some affinity between the off-balance-sheet transactions of a corporate giant such as Enron, which defrauded thousands of workers and investors, and the offline dealings of the terrorist networks about which we hear so much. In a general way, global flows of arms, labor, drugs, and gems rely frequently on high-tech communications and on nonstate means of violence. This is the zone where the violence of terrorism and the independence of various illicit global flows come together.

Yet, the cellularity which characterizes both capital and

international terror has other faces, and I address the ways in which nonstate organizations have been harnessing the means of cellularity to create new solidarities and new strategies to contest the power of nation-state and global corporations in chapter 6 on grassroots globalization. These are utopian cellular forms, devoted to goals of equity, transparency, and inclusion. They are as far from the ethos of terror as one can get. But they too are instances of the new logics of cellularity.

It is of course empirically absurd to speak of the end of the nation-state. But if we examine carefully the proliferation of cellular forms that surround and question the vertebrate morality of the modern system of nation-states, it does seem there is both mutual dependence and antagonism between these two principles of large-scale political attachment and organization. The complementarity and difference between vertebrate and cellular systems give us a structural way to examine the crisis of the nation-state in the era of globalization and force us to see that the forms of global terrorism of which we are most conscious after 9/11 are only instances of a deep and broad transformation in the morphology of global economy and politics.

This broad transformation, of which global terror is the violent and asymmetric edge, may be regarded as a crisis of circulation. That is, it may be seen as a crisis produced by what in my earlier work I called the "disjunctures" between various kinds of flows—of images, ideologies, goods, people, and wealth—that seem to mark the era of globalization (1996). These disjunctures are largely produced by modes and means of circulation which operate with different rhythms in their negotiation of space and time. Sometimes discussed as disjunct global flows, they produce local contradictions and tensions of many kinds. Since all these tensions have something to do with processes of global flow that are not coherently synchronized, they may be termed crises of circulation. In so naming them, we are reminded that globalization has much to do with the movements of finance capital and that Karl Marx was among the first to note that circulation, especially of money in relation to commodities, was vital to the workings and contradictions of capital. Today, building on this Marxian insight, we can recognize that the logics of circulation have grown ever more diverse and disjunct in their spatial scope, semiotic legibility, speed and tempo of movement, and paths through which they move or that they create afresh for their movement.

Returning to the always fragile idea of a world of national economies, we can characterize the current era of globalization—driven by the triple engines of speculative capital, new financial instruments, and high-speed information technologies—as creating new tensions between the wanton urge of global capital to roam without license or limit and the still regnant fantasy that the nation-state assures a sovereign economic space. This new crisis of circulation (more exactly a crisis of the disjunct relations between different paths and forms of circulation) is the broad landscape against which tensions between vertebrate and cellular forms now unfold. This struggle can also be seen in the friction between the forms of circulation and the circulation of forms in the era of globalization.

Though these forms are inextricably intertwined, they are simultaneously prone to clash. But it is not a clash of doctrines, cultures, or civilizations. It is a clash between different modes of large-scale organization — which I have here called cellular and vertebrate — within the ongoing crisis of circulation. Osama bin Laden and Al-Qaeda are terrifying names for this clash, which involves much more than the question of terrorism.

War as Order

A key insight Achille Mbembe (2003) has offered us is that in societies in which everyday life is characterized by the everydayness of physical violence, militarized conflict, and somatic brutality in the name of collective identities, we can no longer imagine a simple opposition between nature and war on one hand and social life and peace on the other. Mbembe invites us to imagine a more terrifying landscape, in which order (regularity, predictability, routine, and everydayness itself) is organized around the fact or the prospect of violence.

The global politics surrounding the image of terror and terrorism after 9/11 press us to take up this invitation in a slightly different way. They break down the division between civilian and military space. The actions of various terrorist networks and agents seek to infuse all of everyday civilian life with fear. They presume a world where civilians do not exist. This is not just total war, as it has been waged by powerful states at different points in history, it is quotidian war, war as an everyday possibility, waged precisely to destabilize the idea that there is an "everyday" for anyone outside the space and time of war. To this, terrorism adds the element of unpredictability, the key to producing constant fear. States that engage in this sort of strategy with respect to their own populations or other populations are rightly viewed as engaged in terrorism itself.

Terror produces its effects by regularly blurring the bounds between the spaces and times of war and peace. It also works by its efforts to disguise its own principles of organization and mobilization. And it is above all devoted to the decimation of order, understood as peace or freedom from violence. Terror, in the name of whatever ideology of equity, liberty, or justice, seeks to install violence as the central regulative principle of everyday life. This is what is terrifying about terror, even beyond its bodily traumas, its spatial promiscuity, its dramas of self-sacrifice, its refusal of reciprocal humanism. Terror is the rightful name for any effort to replace peace with violence as the guaranteed anchor of everyday life. It uses emergency as its routine and values exceptional forms of violence and violation as its norm.

The sort of globalized terror network that we now see in such organizations as Al-Qaeda adds to these logics the capability to globalize through cellular organization. So there is a double sense of nausea and uncertainty that these networks produce. They seek to reverse the relationship between peace and everyday life, and they do so without any need or regard for those principles of vertebrate coordination on which the nation-state has always relied. This is an epistemological assault on us all, for it destabilizes our two most cherished assumptions—that peace is the natural marker of social order and that the nation-state is natural guarantor and container of such order. Terror is thus the nightmarish side of globalization, and we need to look more closely at the logic of this nightmare. For now, let us note that terror in the era of globalization cannot be divorced from certain deeper crises and contradictions that surround the nation-state. One such crisis, taken up in the next chapter, concerns the link between minorities *within* the modern nation-state and the marginalization *of* the nation-state by the forces of globalization.

3 Globalization and Violence

lobalization is a source of debate almost everywhere. It is the name of a new industrial revolution (driven by powerful information and communication technologies) which has barely begun. Because of its newness, it taxes our linguistic resources for understanding it and our political resources for managing it. In the United States and in the ten or so most wealthy countries of the world, globalization is certainly a positive buzzword for corporate elites and their political allies. But for migrants, people of color, and other marginals (the so-called South in the North), it is a source of worry about inclusion, jobs, and deeper marginalization. And the worry of the marginals, as always in human history, is a worry to the elites. In the remaining countries of the world, the underdeveloped and the truly destitute ones, there is a double anxiety: fear of inclusion, on draconian terms, and fear of exclusion, for this seems like exclusion from history itself.

Whether we are in the North or the South, globalization also challenges our strongest tool for making newness manageable, and that is the recourse to history. We can do our best to see globalization as just a new phase (and face) of capitalism, or imperialism, or neocolonialism, or modernization or developmentalism. And there is some force to this hunt for the analogy that will let us tame the beast of globalization in the prison house (or zoo) of language. But this historicizing move (for all of its technical legitimacy) is doomed to fail precisely in accounting for the part of globalization that is unsettling in its newness. Recourse to the archives of prior world systems, old empires, and known forms of power and capital can indeed soothe us, but only up to a point. Beyond that point lurks the intuition of many poor people (and their supporters in the world) that globalization poses some new challenges which cannot be addressed with the comforts of history, even those of the history of bad people and nasty world conquerors. This hazy intuition is at the heart of the uncertain coalitions and uneasy dialogues that surround globalization, even in the streets of Seattle, Prague, Washington, and many other less dramatized locations.

Where exactly does this newness lie and why do many critical intellectuals fail to understand it better? In my opinion, there are three interrelated factors which make globalization difficult to understand in terms of earlier histories of state and market. The first is the role of finance capital (especially in its speculative forms) in the world economy today: it is faster, more multiplicative, more abstract, and more invasive of national economies than ever in its previous history. And because of its loosened links to manufacture and other forms of productive wealth, it is a horse with no apparent structural rider. The second reason has to do with the peculiar power of the information revolution in its electronic forms. Electronic information technologies are part and parcel of the new financial instruments, many of which have technical powers which are clearly ahead of the protocols for their regulation. Thus, whether or not the nation-state is fading out, no one can argue that the idea of a national economy (in the sense first articulated by Friedrich List) is any more an easily sustainable project. Thus, by extension, national sovereignty is now an unsettled project for specific technical reasons of a new sort and scale. Third, the new, mysterious, and almost magical forms of wealth generated by electronic finance markets appear directly responsible for the growing gaps between rich and poor, even in the richest countries in the world.

More importantly, the mysterious roamings of finance capital are matched by new kinds of migration, both elite and proletarian, which create unprecedented tensions between identities of origin, identities of residence, and identities of aspiration for many migrants in the world labor market. Leaky financial frontiers, mobile identities, and fast-moving technologies of communication and transaction together produce debates, both within and across national boundaries, that hold new potentials for violence.

There are many ways that we can approach the problems of globalization and violence. One could take the United States and ask whether the growth in the prison industry (and what is sometimes called the carceral state) is tied to the dynamics of regional economies which are being pushed out of other more humane forms of employment and wealth creation. One could consider Indonesia and ask why there is a deadly increase in intrastate violence between indigenous populations and state-sponsored migrants. One could study Sri Lanka and ask whether there are real links between the incessant civil war there and the global diaspora of Tamils, with such results as eelam.com, an example of cyber-secession (Jeganathan 1998). One could worry about conventional secessionist movements from Chechnya and Kashmir to the Basque Country and many parts of Africa and ask whether their violence is strictly endogenous. One could look at Palestine and ask whether the intimate violence of internal colonialism is now so deeply tied to mass media and global intervention that it is doomed to permanent institutionalization. One could position oneself in Kosovo or Iraq and ask whether the violent humanitarianism of NATO air strikes is the newest form of biblical retribution by the armed gods of our times. Or one could identify with the perspective of terrified minorities in many national spaces, such as Palestine, Timor, or Sierra Leone, often living in detention camps parading as neighborhoods or refugee camps, and ask about the violence of displacement and relocation.

Cutting across all these locations and forms of violence is the presence of some major global factors. The growing and organized violence against women, famously in the Taliban regime, is also clearly evident in many other societies that seek to cast the first stone, such as the United States, where domestic violence remains prevalent. The mobilization of youth armies, notably in Africa but also in many other sites of intrastate warfare, is producing war veterans who have

hardly seen adulthood, much less peace. Child labor is sufficiently troubling as a globalized form of violence against children, but the labor of fighting in civilian militias and military gangs is a particularly deadly form of induction into
violence at an early age. And then there are the more insidious
forms of violence experienced by large numbers of the world's
poor as they undergo displacements by huge dam projects
or by projects of slum clearance. Here they experience the
effects of the global politics of security states as victims of
economic embargos, police violence, ethnic mobilization, and
job losses. The shutdown of small-scale industries in Delhi in
the past decade is a vivid example of the collusion of high-
minded environmental discourses, corrupt city politics, and
the desperate scramble for jobs and livelihood. This is part of
the reason that the poor sometimes subject themselves to the
intimate violence of selling their body parts in global organ
markets, selling their whole bodies to domestic labor in un-
safe countries, and offering their daughters and sons into sex
work and other permanently scarring occupations.

Let us pull back for a moment and consider some objec-
tions to this line of thought. What does this catalogue have to
do with globalization as such? Is it not just one more chapter
in the story of power, greed, corruption, and exclusion that
we can find as far back in human history as we please? I would
argue otherwise. Many of the examples I have cited above are
tied in specific ways to transformations in the world economy
since 1970, to specific battles over indigenism and national
sovereignty produced by the battle between competing uni-
versalisms such as freedom, market, democracy, and rights,

which simply did not operate in the same way in earlier periods. Above all, the many examples I have given fit with the major empirical fact of macroviolence in the past two decades, which is the relative and marked growth in intrastate versus interstate violence. Thus, the maps of states and the maps of warfare no longer fit an older, realist geography. And when we add to this the global circulation of arms, drugs, mercenaries, mafias, and other paraphernalia of violence, it is difficult to keep local instances local in their significance.

Of all these contexts for violence, ranging from the most intimate (such as rape, bodily mutilation, and dismemberment) to the most abstract (such as forced migration and legal minoritization), the most difficult one is the worldwide assault against minorities of all kinds. In this matter, every state (like every family) is unhappy in its own way. But why are we seeing a virtually worldwide genocidal impulse toward minorities, whether they are numerical, cultural, or political minorities and whether they are minorities through lack of the proper ethnicity or proper documentation or by being visible embodiments of some history of mutual violence or abuse? This global pattern requires something of a global answer, and that is the aim of this book.

The existing answers do not take us very far. Is this a clash of civilizations? Not likely, since many of these forms of violence are intracivilizational. Is it a failure of states to fulfill the Weberian norm of monopolizing violence? Partly, but this failure itself requires further explanation, along with the concomitant worldwide growth in "private" armies, security zones, consultants, and bodyguards. Is it a general worldwide numbing of our humanitarian impulses, as someone like Michael Ignatieff may suggest (1998), due to the effect of too many mass media images of faraway wars and ethnocides? Perhaps, but the growth in grassroots coalitions for change, equity, and health on a worldwide basis suggests that the human faculty for long-distance empathy has not yet been depleted. Is it the concomitant growth in a huge global arms traffic which links small arms and Kalashnikovs to the official state-to-state trade in rockets, tanks, and radar systems in a huge and shady range of deals? Yes, but this tells us only about necessary conditions for global violence and not about sufficient ones.

Or are we in the midst of a vast worldwide Malthusian correction, which works through the idioms of minoritization and ethnicization but is functionally geared to preparing the world for the winners of globalization, minus the inconvenient noise of its losers? Is this a vast form of what we may call econocide, a worldwide tendency (no more perfect in its workings than the market) to arrange the disappearance of the losers in the great drama of globalization? A scary scenario but fortunately lacking in plausible evidence, partly because the world's biggest criminals and tyrants have learned the languages of democracy, dignity, and rights.

So what is it about minorities that seems to attract new forms and scales of violence in many different parts of the world? The first step to an answer is that both minorities and majorities are the products of a distinctly modern world of statistics, censuses, population maps, and other tools of state created mostly since the seventeenth century. Minorities and majorities emerge explicitly in the process of developing ideas of number, representation, and electoral franchise in places affected by the democratic revolutions of the eighteenth century, including satellite spaces in the colonial world.

So, minorities are a recent social and demographic category, and today they activate new worries about rights (human and otherwise), about citizenship, about belonging and autochthony, and about entitlements from the state (or its phantom remnants). And they invite new ways of examining the obligations of states as well as the boundaries of political humanity, falling as they do in the uneasy gray area between citizens proper and humanity in general. It is no surprise that humans viewed as insufficient by others (as for example the disabled, the aged, and the sick) are often the first targets of marginalization or cleansing. That Nazi Germany sought to eliminate all of these categories (iconized by the figure of the Jew) is useful to contemplate.

But minorities do not come preformed. They are produced in the specific circumstances of every nation and every nationalism. They are often the carriers of the unwanted memories of the acts of violence that produced existing states, of forced conscription, or of violent extrusion as new states were formed. And, in addition, as weak claimants on state entitlements or drains on the resources of highly contested national resources, they are also reminders of the failures of various state projects (socialist, developmentalist, and capitalist). They are marks of failure and coercion. They are embarrassments to any state-sponsored image of national purity and state fairness. They are thus scapegoats in the classical sense.

But what is the special status of such scapegoats in the era of globalization? After all, strangers, sick people, nomads, religious dissidents, and similar minor social groups have always been targets of prejudice and xenophobia. Here I suggest a single and simple hypothesis. Given the systemic compromise of national economic sovereignty that is built into the logic of globalization, and given the increasing strain this puts on states to behave as trustees of the interests of a territorially defined and confined "people," minorities are the major site for displacing the anxieties of many states about their own minority or marginality (real or imagined) in a world of a few megastates, of unruly economic flows and compromised sovereignties. Minorities, in a word, are metaphors and reminders of the betrayal of the classical national project. And it is this betrayal—actually rooted in the failure of the nation-state to preserve its promise to be the guarantor of national sovereignty—that underwrites the worldwide impulse to extrude or to eliminate minorities. And this also explains why state military forces are often involved in intrastate ethnocide.

Of course, every case of internal violence against minorities also has its own realist sociology of rising expectations, cruel markets, corrupt state agencies, arrogant interventions from the outside, and deep histories of internal hate and suspicion waiting to be mobilized. But these only account for the characters. We need to look elsewhere for the plot. And the plot—worldwide in its force—is a product of the justified fear that the real world game has escaped the net of state sovereignty and interstate diplomacy.

And yet, why are minorities targets of this worldwide pattern? Here we may return to the classic anthropological argument by Mary Douglas that "dirt is matter out of place" and that all moral and social taxonomies find abhorrent the items that blur their boundaries (1966). Minorities of the sort that I have described—the infirm, the religiously deviant, the disabled, the mobile, the illegal, and the unwelcome in the space of the nation-state—blur the boundaries between "us" and "them," here and there, in and out, healthy and unhealthy, loyal and disloyal, needed but unwelcome. This last binary is the key to the puzzle. In one way or the other, we need the "minor" groups in our national spaces—if nothing else to clean our latrines and fight our wars. But they are surely also unwelcome because of their anomalous identities and attachments. And in this double quality they embody the core problem of globalization itself for many nation-states: it is both necessary (or at least unavoidable) and it is unwelcome. It is both us (we can own it, control it, and use it, in the optimistic vision) and not us (we can avoid it, reject it, live without it, deny it, and eliminate it, in the pessimistic vision). Thus, from this point of view, the globalization of violence against minorities enacts a deep anxiety about the national project and its own ambiguous relationship to globalization. And globalization, being a force without a face, cannot be the object of ethnocide. But minorities can.

Put more generally, and this is an argument more fully elaborated in chapter 4, minorities are the flash point for a series of uncertainties that mediate between everyday life and its fast-shifting global backdrop. They create uncertainties about the national self and national citizenship because of their mixed status. Their legally ambiguous status puts pressures on constitutions and legal orders. Their movements threaten the policing of borders. Their financial transactions blur the lines between national economies and between legal and criminal transactions. Their languages exacerbate worries about national cultural coherence. Their lifestyles are easy ways to displace widespread tensions in society, especially in urban society. Their politics tend to be multifocal, so they are always sources of anxiety to security states. When they are wealthy, they raise the specter of elite globalization, working as its pariah mediators. And when they are poor, they are convenient symbols of the failure of many forms of development and welfare. Above all, since almost all ideas of nation and peoplehood rely on some idea of ethnic purity or singularity and the suppression of the memories of plurality, ethnic minorities blur the boundaries of national peoplehood. This uncertainty, exacerbated by the inability of many states to secure national economic sovereignty in the era of globalization, can translate into a lack of tolerance of any sort of collective stranger.

It is difficult to know who might emerge as the target minority, the ill-fated stranger. In some cases it seems obvious, in others less so. And that is because minorities are not born but made, historically speaking. In short, it is through specific choices and strategies, often of state elites or political leaders, that particular groups, who have stayed invisible, are rendered visible as minorities against whom campaigns of calumny can be unleashed, leading to explosions of ethnocide. So, rather than saying that minorities produce violence, we could better say that violence, especially at the national level, requires minorities. And this production of minorities requires unearthing some histories and burying others. This process is what accounts for the complex ways in which global issues and clashes gradually "implode" into nations and localities, often in the form of paroxysmal violence in the name of some majority. One classic case is the process by which the Sikhs in India were gradually turned into a problematic minority (Axel 2001). This was not the outcome of any simple form of census politics. It was based on a long twentieth century of regional and national politics and was finally produced in the violence of 1984, the assassination of Indira Gandhi, the state's counterinsurgency campaign against Sikh separatists, and the carnage of the 1984 riots in Delhi and elsewhere. It could be argued that it was in fact the massive unleashing of state and popular violence against Sikhs in 1984 that produced the Sikhs as a cultural and political minority, whose own small terrorist component acquired a general sacrality after these events. So, within a century (and some would say within a decade) a category that was considered a militant auxiliary of the Hindu world turned into its most dangerous internal enemy for at least a decade after 1984.

Consider one last reflection on the links between globalization and violence against minorities. This connection forces one to perform the hardest of analytic exercises, which is to show how forces of great speed, scale, and scope (i.e., the processes of globalization), which are also in many ways very abstract, can be connected to bodily violence of the most intimate sort, framed by the familiarity of everyday relations, the comfort of neighborhood, and the bonds of intimacy. How can friend kill friend, neighbor kill neighbor, even kinsman kill kinsman? These new forms of intimate violence seem especially puzzling in an era of fast technologies, abstract financial instruments, remote forms of power, and large-scale flows of techniques and ideologies.

One way to unravel the horror of the worldwide growth in intimate bodily violence in the context of increased abstraction and circulation of images and technologies is to consider that the relationship is not paradoxical at all. The body, especially the minoritized body, can simultaneously be the mirror and the instrument of those abstractions we fear most. Minorities and their bodies are, after all, the products of high degrees of abstraction in counting, classifying, and surveying populations. So, the body of the historically produced minority combines the seductions of the familiar and the reductions of the abstract in social life, allowing fears of the global to be embodied within it and, when specific situations become overcharged with anxiety, for that body to be annihilated. To be sure, we need to understand a great many specific events and processes in order to get from the vertiginous spin of the global to the intimate heat of local violence. But here is the possibility to consider: that part of the effort to slow down the whirl of the global and its seeming largeness of reach is by holding it still, and making it small, in the body of the violated minor. Such violence, in this perspective, is not about old hatreds and primordial fears. It is an effort to exorcise the new, the emergent, and the uncertain, one name for which is globalization.

The relationship of the categories of majority and minority, especially in liberal democracies, is slippery and volatile. Their special relationship to globalized violence is more closely examined in the following chapter.

4 Fear of Small Numbers

T here is a basic puzzle surrounding rage about minorities in a globalizing world. The puzzle is about why the relatively small numbers that give the word minority its most simple meaning and usually imply political and military weakness do not prevent minorities from being objects of fear and of rage. Why kill, torture, or ghettoize the weak? This may be a relevant question for ethnic violence against small groups at any time in history (Hinton 2002). Here, I seek to engage this puzzle with special reference to the era of globalization, especially from the late 1980s until the present.

Fear of the Weak

The comparative historical question does not, in any case, apply to all of human history, since minorities and majorities are recent historical inventions, essentially tied up with ideas about nations, populations, representation, and enumeration which are no more than a few centuries old. They are also today *universal* ideas, since the techniques of counting, classification, and political participation that underlie the ideas of majority and minority are everywhere associated with the modern nation-state.

The idea of a majority is not prior to or independent from that of a minority, especially in the discourses of modern politics. Majorities are as much the product of enumeration and political nomination as are minorities. Indeed, majorities need minorities in order to exist, even more than the reverse.

Hence, the first step toward addressing why the weak, in so many ethnonationalist settings, are feared, is to go back to the "we/they" question in elementary sociological theory. In this theory, the creation of collective others, or them's, is a requirement, through the dynamics of stereotyping and identity contrast, for helping to set boundaries and mark off the dynamics of the we. This aspect of the theory of the scapegoat, the stereotype, and the other grows out of that brand of symbolic interactionism that was made explicit in the works of Cooley and Mead, but it is also entirely central to the core of Freud's understanding of group dynamics, including his classic essay on the narcissism of minor differences (which I discuss later in the chapter).

In this sociological tradition, the understanding of the process of we-making is limited, since it is seen as a mechanical by-product of the process by which theys are created. The process requires simple contrasts and sharp boundaries which help to consolidate "we" identities. The making of we's, of collective selves, is given short shrift in this tradition, since it is regarded as sociologically natural and unrequiring of deeper thought. Mainstream sociological theory, especially in regard to group formation, does explore the role of conflict (as in the tradition of Simmel) or of religion (in the tradition of Durkheim) or of antagonistic interest (as in the tradition of Marx) in the building of collective identities. But even though these traditions do cast some light on the formation of we identities as a partially independent process, without reference to the we/they dialectic, they do not tend to be deeply reflective about the formation of what I have elsewhere called "predatory identities" (2000a).

Predatory Identities

I define as predatory those identities whose social construction and mobilization require the extinction of other, proximate social categories, defined as threats to the very existence of some group, defined as a we. Predatory identities emerge, periodically, out of pairs of identities, sometimes sets that are larger than two, which have long histories of close contact, mixture, and some degree of mutual stereotyping. Occasional violence may or may not be parts of these histories, but some degree of contrastive identification is always involved. One of these pairs or sets of identities often turns predatory by mobilizing an understanding of itself as a threatened majority. This kind of mobilization is the key step in turning a benign social identity into a predatory identity.

The formation of an ethnos into a modern nation often provides the basis for the emergence of predatory identities, identities that claim to require the extinction of another collectivity for their own survival. Predatory identities are almost always majoritarian identities. That is, they are based on claims about, and on behalf of, a threatened majority. In fact, in many instances, they are claims about cultural majorities that seek to be exclusively or exhaustively linked with the identity of the nation. Sometimes these claims are made in terms of religious majorities, such as Hindus, Christians, or Jews, and at other times in terms of linguistic, racial, or other sorts of majorities, such as Germans, Indians, or Serbs. The discourse of these mobilized majorities often has within it the idea that it could be itself turned into a minority unless another minority disappears, and for this reason, predatory groups often use pseudo-demographic arguments about rising birthrates among their targeted minority enemies. Thus, predatory identities arise in those circumstances in which majorities and minorities can plausibly be seen as being in danger of trading places. This inner reciprocity is a central feature of this analysis and will be revisited below in this chapter.

Predatory identities emerge in the tension between majority identities and national identities. Identities may be described as "majoritarian" not simply when they are invoked by objectively larger groups in a national polity but when they strive to close the gap between the majority and the purity of the national whole. This is a key point about the conditions under which identities turn predatory. Majority identities that successfully mobilize what I earlier defined as the *anxiety of incompleteness* about their sovereignty can turn predatory. Incompleteness, in this sense, is not only about effective control or practical sovereignty but more importantly about purity and its relationship to identity.

In the previous chapter I referred to Mary Douglas's contributions to the subject of purity and categorical identity. Her insights can be extended to note that predatory identities, especially when they are associated with majoritarianism, thrive in the gap between the sense of numerical majority and the fantasy of national purity and wholeness. Predatory identities, in other words, are products of situations in which the idea of a national peoplehood is successfully reduced to the principle of ethnic singularity, so that the existence of even the smallest minority within national boundaries is seen as an intolerable deficit in the purity of the national whole. In such circumstances, the very idea of being a majority is a frustration, since it implies some sort of ethnic diffusion of the national peoplehood. Minorities, being a reminder of this small but frustrating deficit, thus unleash the urge to purify. This is one basic element of an answer to the question: why can small numbers excite rage? Small numbers represent a tiny obstacle between majority and totality or total purity. In a sense, the smaller the number and the weaker the minority, the deeper the rage about its capacity to make a majority feel like a mere majority rather than like a whole and uncontested ethnos.

The most remarked twentieth century example of this sense of frustrated purity is, of course, the mobilization of "Germanness" as a predatory identity by the Nazis, directed especially but not exclusively against the Jews. Many scholars have forcefully argued that especially for the assimilated Jewish members of the German bourgeoisie, it was possible, even well into the period of Nazi power, to believe that they were Jewish in an entirely secondary sense and that they were in every important regard fully German. Conversely, it is possible to argue that far from being a successful mobilization of a continuous, unchanging, nationally coded feature of the German people, anti-Semitism had to be regularly mobilized and reawakened through powerful campaigns of racial and political propaganda, through which Jews could be seen as non-Germans and anti-Germans. The special contribution of Nazis to the complex traditions of European anti-Semitism has been identified by some important scholars to be the infusion of scientific racism and its accompanying eugenic and demographic ideas to earlier forms of religious and social stereotyping.

Even Daniel Goldhagen (1996), who otherwise creates a remarkably racialized picture of the identities of "ordinary Germans," concedes that the Nazis made critical new contributions to the definition and mobilization of Germanness as the identity of a threatened majority, threatened especially by the racial cancer (also a Nazi trope) of the Jews. Whatever the status of Goldhagen's arguments about what he called "eliminationist anti-Semitism" and its mobilization among the vast majority of ordinary Germans, the major weakness of the book is its refusal to recognize its own massive evidence, not so much of a deep, primordial, and hardwired form of anti-Semitism among all Germans, successfully captured by the Nazis for the project of eliminating all Jews from the face of the earth, but of the extraordinary amount of energy that was required to turn many German nationals into instruments of the Final Solution.

The huge apparatus of Nazi media and spectacle, the tireless circulation of racialized propaganda and officially circulated rumors, and the self-fulfilling performances (in which degraded Jewish populations were seen as evidence of the subhuman qualities of Jews) were a remarkable feat of active ideological and political engineering. Even in themselves they could be seen as evidence of the effort required to build a successful national consensus in favor of the campaign against Jews as a central platform of the Third Reich. One could also argue that the engagement of civilians of various kinds in police battalions, death camps, and forced marches, which were part of the machinery of the Final Solution, were themselves among the massive political performatives through which Jews were successfully rendered subhuman and those Germans who were directly involved were drawn, by violent action, into the consensus about Jews as national filth.

There is a great deal more that could be said about Nazi anti-Semitism and the larger national project of National Socialism. For the purposes of this argument, the main point is that once the project of Germanness became defined in ethno-racial terms and the logic of purity came into play, a variety of minorities became sites of rage about incomplete purity: homosexuals, the aged and infirm, Gypsies, and, above all, Jews. Jews were painted in Nazi propaganda as representing various kinds of social, political, and economic threats, but they were above all seen as a cancer, as a problem for the purity of German-Aryan blood, for the almost perfect project of a nationally pure and untainted ethnos. German identity, as mobilized by the Nazis, required the complete elimination of Jews from the German social body, and since the German project was a project of world dominion, it required their elimination worldwide.

The Nazi project of eliminating many minorities from the earth also casts light on another aspect of the way predatory identities are mobilized. In this case, perhaps for the first time in the history of humanity, two contradictory impulses were mobilized in the project of genocide. The first was the mechanical, technological, and bureaucratic side of the project, captured in Hannah Arendt's memorable phrase about "the banality of evil" (Arendt 1963). The second, however, is the degradation, abuse, and horrifyingly intimate violence that was wreaked by German soldiers, conscripts, camp guards, militias, and ordinary citizens at every level and in every site of the Final Solution. This is the contradictory intimacy generated by predatory identities. One way to understand this contradiction is that reducing target populations to subhuman states facilitates the work of large-scale murder by creating distance between killers and killed and by providing a self-fulfilling proof of the ideological argument that the victims are subhuman, vermin, insects, scum, garbage, and yet a cancerous part of the valued national body.

Yet there is more to the degradation that frequently accompanies large-scale genocidal violence. I would suggest that it is precisely the smallness of the gap between national totality and minority presence that produces the anxiety of incompleteness and creates the frustration and rage that drives those forms of degradation that shock us most, from Nazi Germany to Rwanda, from Kosovo to Mumbai. Again we must review some arguments about the narcissism of small differences, which I do later in the chapter.

The Nazi example might appear to be an extreme case that has little in common with such recent liberal majoritarianisms as those of India, Pakistan, Britain, or Germany (among others), all of which are more open to social difference than the Nazis were. The Hindutva ideology in India, for example, the "sons of the soil" ideology in Malaysia, or various ideologies of citizenship in Europe might be seen as liberal majoritarianisms, that is, as majoritarianisms which seek to be inclusive. Are these majoritarianisms fundamentally different from the more "totalitarian" ones that the Nazis installed in Germany in the 1930s and 1940s? My suggestion is that all majoritarianisms have in them the seeds of genocide, since they are invariably connected with ideas about the singularity and completeness of the national ethnos.

The difficult question is to assess how and under what conditions liberal majoritarianisms might turn illiberal and potentially genocidal. When does the fact of incomplete national purity become susceptible to translation and mobilization in the service of building a predatory identity? There are two ways of answering this question without entering into an elaborate empiricist study of causes, conditions, and comparisons. One is to suggest that liberal thought has a fundamental ambivalence about the legitimacy of collectivities as political actors and, as a result, is always open to the manipulation of arguments about quality disguised as arguments about quantity. This approach is explored below in this chapter.

The second is a more generally historical and tentative answer to the question of when the condition of incomplete purity propels an argument for genocide. The historical ingredients for this transformation or tipping point appear to include the following: the capture of the state by parties or other groups that have placed their political bets on some sort of racialized nationalist ideology; the availability of census tools and techniques that encourage enumerated communities to become norms for the idea of community itself; a felt lack of fit between political borders and community migrations and populations, yielding a new alertness to politically abandoned ethnic kin or to ethnic strangers claiming to be one's kinsmen; and a successful campaign of fear, directed at numerical majorities, which convinces them that they are at risk of destruction by minorities, who know how to use the law (and the entire apparatus of liberal-democratic politics) to advance their special ends. To these factors, globalization adds its specific energies, which are discussed at the end of this chapter. This set of factors is not intended to be exhaustive or predictive. It is intended to suggest that the Nazi project may have been extraordinary in its consistency and the reach of its genocidal imagination. But as an ideology of majoritarianism turned predatory, it does not allow us to imagine that liberalism is immune from the conditions that produce majoritarian genocide. India in the past two decades is a prime case of the latter possibility.

The Nazi case certainly invites us to see how predatory

identities are formed and to recognize that the reflexive theory of the other, in which scapegoats (often minorities) are viewed as a functional requirement for the building up of feelings of we-ness, is both mechanical and partial. The mobilization of feelings of we-ness, especially in the strong form that I have here called predatory, depends on the tension between ideas of the sacred wholeness of the national demos and the statistical idea of a majority. Majoritarianism thrives where majorities become seized of the fantasy of national purity, in that zone where quantity meets — but does not completely define — quality. This issue opens up another dimension of the problem of small numbers, which is the link between number, quantity, and political voice.

Number in the Liberal Imagination

Numbers have an ambivalent place in liberal social theory, and the relationship between numbers and categories is today at the heart of some central tensions between liberal social theory and democratic norms. The issue of majorities in the modern nation-state allows us to examine these tensions in a productive manner. From a certain point of view, the critical number, for liberal social theory, is the number one, which is the numerical sign of the individual. Insofar as the individual is at the normative heart of liberalism and is shared ground even among competing liberalisms, the number "one" is the smallest important number for liberalism. As the smallest integer, the number "one" has a number of properties of interest to mathematicians, but for liberal social theory, it is in some sense the only important number, other than zero. The number zero is almost as important because it is the key to converting integers into numbers in the hundreds, the thousands, the millions, and so on. In other words, zero is the numerical key to the idea of the masses, which is one of the categories around which liberal and democratic thought part ways. Lenin is quoted as having said: "Politics is where the masses are, not where there are thousands but where there are millions, that is where serious politics begins" (Merton and Sills 2001).

Much liberal thought imagines large groups as aggregations of individuals (that is, of infinite combinations of the number one). A significant part of the utilitarian tradition in liberal thought, from Bentham to Rawls, tries to imagine collective life as organized around forms of aggregate decision making which privilege the individual or a number of persons no larger than one. In this way, liberal thought, in terms of theories of representation, of the collective good, and of social science, imagines aggregations of individuals as constituted by the addition of large sets of the number one. Put another way, the appearance of collectivities, in the central traditions of liberal thought, is a matter of the aggregation of singular interests and agents seeking solutions to the fact that they are forced to interact with one another. This is, of course, only a way of restating the standard characterizations of market models in neoclassical economics and of the images of collective life that lie behind them. In this sense, liberal thought imagines collectivities to be social forms whose logics, motives, and dynamism can always be inferred from some method for understanding the aggregation of interested individuals.

For liberal thought, from its very beginnings, the problem about democracy is the possibility that it could encourage the political legitimacy of large numbers. The sharp contrast between the people and the masses is constituted in liberal thought around what happens to the number "one" when many zeros are added to it. The idea of the masses (as in Ortega y Gasset's classic book, *The Revolt of the Masses*) is associated in liberal thought with large numbers that have lost the rationalities embedded in the individual, in the number one. Thus, the masses are always seen as the product and the basis of fascism and totalitarianism, both because of the sense of their being composed of nonindividuals (or individuals who had lost their mental capabilities to exercise their own rational interests) and of the sense of a collectivity orchestrated by forces outside itself, such as a state, a dictator, or a myth which was not produced by the deliberative interaction between individuals. The quotation from Lenin captures precisely what liberal thought fears about large numbers. It is because of this potential affinity between large numbers and the birth of the masses that much liberal thought has rightly been characterized by a fear of large numbers. This much seems intuitively clear. But where then does the fear of *small* numbers come in?

Except for the number one, which is a special case, small numbers are troubling to liberal social thought for a variety of reasons. First, small numbers are associated with oligopolies, elites, and tyrannies. They suggest the possibility of what today is called "elite capture" of resources, privileges, and the very capacity to mediate. Small numbers are also a worry because they raise the specter of conspiracy, of the cell, the spy, the traitor, the dissident, or the revolutionary. Small numbers introduce the intrusion of the private into the public sphere, and with it the associated dangers of nepotism, collusion, subversion, and deception. They harbor the potential for secrecy and privacy, both anathema to the ideas of publicity and transparency that are vital to liberal ideas of rational communication and open deliberation.

More broadly, small numbers always carry the possibility of what in the liberal vernacular of the United States are called "special interests" and thus pose threats to some idea of the "general interest," which is believed to be best served when individuals deliberate or negotiate as individuals with *all other individuals* in the polity, through some legible mechanism of representation.

Minorities are the only powerful instance of small numbers which excite sympathy rather than distrust in the liberal imagination, and that is because they incarnate that numerical smallness of which the prime case is the number one, the individual. So once liberal thought becomes intimately connected to electoral democracy and to deliberative procedures in legislation, the idea of the minority acquires a powerful valence (as with the great regard shown for minority opinions in the U.S. Supreme Court). In fact, the idea of a minority is in its political genealogy not an ethical or cultural idea but a procedural one, having to do with dissenting opinions in deliberative or legislative contexts in a democratic framework.

Thus, in the history of liberal thought, the positive interest in minorities and their opinions has much to do with dissent and little to do with difference. This distinction is an important contributor to the contemporary fear of minorities and requires careful examination.

Dissent and Difference in Contemporary Politics

The initial positive value attached to minorities in Western liberal thought is fundamentally procedural. It has to do with the valuation of rational debate, of the right to dissent, of the value of dissent as a sign of the larger value of free speech and opinion, and of the freedom to express dissenting opinions on matters of public moment without fear of retribution. The U.S. Constitution is perhaps the best place to examine the centrality of dissent to the very idea of freedom. But if we are not careful, we are likely to reverse the course of history and place a relatively recent development, what we may call *substantive* dissent (for example, the right to express even morally monstrous opinions, the right to criticize the policies of the state, or the right to question the religious opinions of the majority) from what we may call *procedural* dissent, which is the original context for the positive value placed on minorities, and especially on minority opinion. The key word here is opinion, for procedural minorities are not cultural or social minorities, they are temporary minorities, minorities solely by and of opinion. Social and cultural minorities, what we may call substantive minorities, are permanent minorities, minorities that have become social and not just procedural.

If we look at the history of Western laws and ideas pertaining to minorities, they take on their full liberal force largely after the birth of the United Nations and in the various conventions pertaining to human rights that are produced after the birth of the United Nations. Of course, there are various piecemeal ideas about the protection of minorities before the formation of the United Nations, but it is only in the second half of the twentieth century, as the idea of human rights became the major currency for negotiating international agreements about the elementary entitlements of all humanity, that substantive social minorities became critical foci of constitutional and political concern in many democracies throughout the world. The rights of minorities, seen under the larger rubric of human rights, acquired a remarkably wide credibility during this period, and, in different national settings, became the basis for major juridical and constitutional struggles over citizenship, justice, political participation, and equality.

This process, in which social and cultural minorities became universally seen as bearers of real or potential rights, conceals a poorly theorized, even unanticipated, transfer of normative value from procedural minorities and temporary minorities to substantive minorities, which often became permanent social and cultural collectivities.

This unintended displacement of the liberal concern with protecting the opinions of procedural minorities (such as minorities on courts, councils, parliaments, and other deliberative bodies) onto the rights of permanent cultural minorities is an important source of the current, deep ambivalence about minorities in democracies of all varieties. The many debates about multiculturalism in the United States and Europe, about subordinate nationalities in various parts of the ex-Soviet Union, about secularism in India, about "sons-of-the-soil" in many countries in Asia, about "autochthony" in many regions of Africa, and about the rights of "indigenous people" throughout Latin America and in places as far apart as New Zealand, Canada, Australia, and Hawaii are different in important ways. But they have in common a concern about the rights of cultural minorities in relation to national states and various cultural majorities, and they always involve struggles over cultural rights as they relate to national citizenship and issues of belonging. In many cases, these struggles have been directly related to the emergence of predatory ethnic identities and of successful efforts to mobilize majorities in projects of ethnic cleansing or ethnocide. These conflicts accelerated during the 1980s and 1990s, during which many nation-states had to simultaneously negotiate two pressures: the pressure to open up their markets to foreign investment, commodities, and images and the pressure to manage the capacity of their own cultural minorities to use the globalized language of human rights to argue for their own claims for cultural dignity and recognition. This dual pressure was a distinctive feature of the 1990s and produced a crisis in many countries for the sense of national boundaries, national sovereignty, and the purity of the national ethnos, and it is directly responsible for the growth of majoritarian racisms in societies as diverse as Sweden and Indonesia as well as Romania, Rwanda, and India.

Muslims in India: Appeasement and Purity

The case of India is instructive in regard to the argument about substantive and procedural minorities that I have been developing. The Indian nation-state was formed in 1947 through a political partition that also produced Pakistan as a new nation-state, formed as a political haven for the Muslims who lived in Britain's Indian Empire. There is a huge and contentious scholarship surrounding the story of Partition, the politics that led to it, and the bizarre geographies it produced (with East and West Pakistan flanking an independent India from 1947 to 1973 when East Pakistan succeeded in seceding from West Pakistan, giving birth to Bangladesh, a new nation on India's eastern borders). I will not take up this politics here, except to note that it produced a permanent state of war between India and Pakistan; spawned the apparently unsolvable crisis of Kashmir; created an alibi for the identification of India's Muslim citizens with its major cross-border enemy, Pakistan; and laid the groundwork for India's current crisis of secularism.

The story of this crisis is also too complex to be told here. What is noteworthy is that as Hinduism and its political mobilizers evolved a cultural politics in the course of the nineteenth and twentieth centuries, the birth of Pakistan created a new link between the Hindu sense of we-ness, the constitutional concern about the rights of minorities, and the rise of a major Hindu political coalition to power in the 1990s. This coalition, of political parties and various affiliated social movements (sometimes called the Sangh Parivar), is virtually coterminous with India's exposure to the pressures of globalization, and it has been bracketed by two of the most horrendous attacks against Muslims in India since the massacres of the Partition: the destruction of the Babri Masjid, a Muslim mosque in North India in 1992, preceded and followed by a wave of genocidal riots against Muslim populations throughout India, and the murderous pogrom against Muslims in the state of Gujarat in 2002. The decade that is bracketed by these events also witnessed the national consolidation of a large body of Indian public opinion, including those of its educated and once-liberal middle classes, against the inclusive, pluralist, and secularist ideals of the Indian constitution and of Nehru, India's first, most charismatic, prime minister. In its place, the coalition of grassroots movements and political parties, led by the Indian People's Party (the Bharatiya Janata Party or BJP), succeeded in creating a deep link between the memory of Hindu humiliations by the pre-British Muslim rulers of India, the dubious patriotism of India's Muslim citizens, the known wish of Pakistan to destroy India militarily, and the growth in militant actions by Muslim terrorists connected with anti-Indian aspirations in the contested state of Kashmir.

Much scholarly and journalistic attention has been paid to this remarkable story in which the world's largest democracy, born with a constitution that pays remarkable attention to religious inclusion, secular tolerance for religious difference, and a general concern with protecting the "weaker sections" of society, could, within forty years of its birth, have turned into an aggressively Hinduized polity, which repeatedly and systematically sought to identify India with Hindus and patriotism with Hindutva (Hindu-ness). This Indian development casts a particular light on the fear of minorities that is worth examining in some detail.

My argument needs to recognize, at this stage, a major interruption from the world of political events. Since the first draft of this paper was written in October 2003 and revised in August 2004, a momentous and unexpected electoral event occurred in India. The Hindu right-wing coalition, led by the BJP, was resoundingly defeated in the recent general elections, and a new coalition, led by the Congress Party of the Nehrus, is back in power. This extraordinary democratic revolution, not the first in the history of independent India, has shocked even the canniest political pundits (not unlike the fall of the Soviet Union in 1989). Though the significance of this major change is still being digested by the experts, there is general agreement among most analysts that the defeat of the BJP coalition expressed two messages. One was that the Indian electorate (both rural and urban) was fed up with the message of Hindutva and did not see it as any substitute for plans and policies concerning the economy and everyday politics at the local level. The second was that the bottom half of the Indian electorate (both rural and urban) was also fed up with seeing the benefits of globalization being consumed by a small group in the ongoing circus of state corruption and elite consumption, with few tangible benefits for themselves. In other words, callous globalization and cynical anti-Muslim mobilization were no longer viable platforms for a national coalition. So we have another novel moment in Indian politics, where the Congress and its allies steer a difficult course between economic justice and global markets and between localized and caste-based politics and a larger, postethnic and pluralist politics.

But it remains crucial to ask why many of India's political parties, a significant part of its population, and a shocking number of cosmopolitan, liberal intellectuals turned to the Hindutva message in the period between 1985 and 2004, a historical period which covers a third of India's history as an independent nation. And the question is not simply historical or academic. The forces of Hindu majoritarianism have not simply disappeared, and its methods, values, and techniques are still very much alive in the Indian polity. We are in a moment of respite, and in order to ensure that the Hinduization of Indian politics remains history, we need to think through this period with as much care as we can summon.

The rise of the Hindu Right as India's major and majoritarian political coalition and its capture of mainstream national opinion largely in the 1980s, after decades of being a fragmented and marginal set of political movements, was connected to four major developments that relate to the issue of numbers and minorities. Each of these developments has something instructive to say about other nations and locations elsewhere in the world.

The first development had to do with minorities that are linked to global movements, identities, and networks. Muslims in India have always been subject to the charge of being more loyal to the wider Muslim world than to India, and their alleged sentimental links to Pakistan (often strenuously repudiated by Indian Muslims) have always been read in the context of the resources and political aspirations of global Islam. In India in the 1980s, the Hindu Right took a special interest in the flow of resources from the Muslim Middle East to religious and educational institutions in India, arguing that this sort of subsidy of Indian Muslims needed to be monitored and restricted and that it justified a controversial policy of reconversions undertaken by the Hindu Right, especially among poorer rural and tribal populations, alleged to have been duped into conversion by the forces of global Islam.

Such reconversions were also instituted with Indian Christian communities and remain a major platform for the grassroots violence and political strategy of the Hindu Right today. In its early manifestations in the 1980s, this battle of conversions was underwritten by the invocation of the size, power, and influence of global Islamic interests and forces, which were seen as the Trojans hidden within the relatively small number of Muslims in Indian communities. Thus, to put the matter crudely, the relatively small numbers of Muslims in India were seen as a mask for the large numbers of Muslims around the world. Today, this picture of militant, transnational Islam has become virtually naturalized in the discourse of Islamic terrorism, especially in the wake of 9/11.

In the Indian case, this picture of Indian Muslims as instruments (and objects) of global Islamic movements (usually portrayed as violent, antinational, and anti-Hindu) was supported by the ongoing commitment of Indian Muslims to going on the Haj (a specially sacred pilgrimage to Mecca, seen as a desirable action at least once in the life of any devout

Muslim) and by the growing traffic between Indian workers (of all kinds and classes) and the oil-rich sheikdoms of the Middle East, especially Saudi Arabia, Dubai, Kuwait, and Bahrain, starting in the 1980s. Among these migrants to the Persian Gulf was a significant number of Indian Muslims, though there is little sign that this was anything other than an economic option for them. Nevertheless, the traffic between India and the Gulf was the site of a great deal of moral and political anxiety which expressed itself in such bureaucratic innovations as the creation of the office of "The Protector of Immigrants," a government agency designed to ensure that Indian workers were not being exported to the Gulf for immoral or fraudulent reasons. In a related moral drama, there was a great deal of attention paid to the growing practice of marriages arranged between richer (and often older) Arab men from the Gulf and Muslim women (often very young) from poor families in impoverished Muslim communities in cities such as Hyderabad, Lucknow, and Agra. This picture of Muslim male depravity and polygamy, targeting the already exploited community of Muslim women, was circulated in the popular press and in such commercial films as *Baazaar*, which were calculated to excite the worst stereotypes of this marriage market. It is highly likely that these commercial and popular images of the abuse of poor Indian Muslim women by decadent Arab men and money lay behind the celebrated legal controversy surrounding a Muslim woman called Shah Bano, who sued her husband for support after he divorced and abandoned her, in accordance with Muslim personal law (one subset of the specialized body of law applicable to many aspects of family and civil life for different religious communities in India) (Das 1990).

The Shah Bano case, which was one of the most publicized legal dramas in India after independence, pitted the state against the judiciary, Hindus against Muslims, feminists against each other, secularists against traditionalists. It also created a deep and harmful opposition between the interests of women and those of minorities (since Shah Bano's appeal was against the customary family laws of her own community). The case showed every sign of rocking the stability of the regime of Rajiv Gandhi, the then prime minister of India, who represented the Nehruvian tradition of secularism and even-handedness toward all religious communities. The Hindu Right, led by the then rising BJP, exploited the Shah Bano case mercilessly, painting themselves as the true protectors of the abused Muslim woman and of women's rights generally, while using the public interest in the case to disseminate vicious messages about the authoritarian power of the Muslim community over its women and the generalized sexual immorality and irresponsibility of Muslim males. The case was eventually resolved through a series of legal and political compromises, but it created a major public doubt about the benefits of secularism and laid some of the grounds for the bizarre idea that the Hindu Right was a more responsible protector of Muslim women's rights than anybody else. It also laid the foundations for a debate, unresolved right up to the present, about the desirability of a Uniform Civil Code (UCC), which is now seen as problematic by most political parties and progressive women's groups but is actively supported by the

Hindu Right, for which it is a major vehicle for Hinduizing the personal law of all minority communities.

The Shah Bano case points up the ways in which issues surrounding minorities, in a complex multireligious democracy like India, can become flash points for fundamental debates about gender, equality, legality, the boundaries of state power, and the ability of religious communities to police themselves. The point here is that small numbers can unsettle big issues, especially in countries like India, where the rights of minorities are directly connected to larger arguments about the role of the state, the limits of religion, and the nature of civil rights as matters of legitimate cultural difference.[1] In a very different context, India's long history of actions and litigations concerning affirmative or remedial action, in the context of the scheduled castes, produced the national convulsions over the 1980 report of the Mandal Commission, which sought to give teeth to a policy of job reservations for castes considered to have been historically the victims of discrimination. The Hindu Right recognized the tension in the rise of the lower castes, signaled by the Mandal Report, and was active in its efforts to take advantage of the rage of the Hindu upper castes, who saw themselves as threatened anew by the political aspirations of their poorer fellow Hindus. Many scholars have pointed out that the Hindu Right, throughout the 1980s, mobilized the politics of the Masjid (the Mosque) against those of Mandal (the intra-Hindu battle over reserved jobs for lower castes). It has also been noted that the effort to create a unified Hindu caste front, in the face of the caste battles unleashed by the Mandal Report, made the Muslim minority a perfect "other" in the production of a mobilized Hindu majority. Most important for the issue of numbers, Amrita Basu, a distinguished student of the politics of communal violence in North India, has observed that the idea of a Hindu majority actually hides the numerical minority of upper caste, landed Hindu castes who have much more to fear from the rise of the lower castes than they have to fear from Muslims in their own localities (Basu 1994). When we place this concern against the general politicization and mass mobilization of the lower castes in public politics throughout India, arguably the single greatest transformation in the political landscape of India over the past half century (Jaffrelot 2003), we can see that the fear of small numbers is further inflected by the Hindu minority which actually has the most to gain from the cultural fiction of a Hindu majority.

The Hindu majority is a double fiction in contemporary India, first because the category "Hindu" is unthinkable in contemporary politics apart from its birth in colonial ethnographies and census categories and second because the deep divisions between upper and lower castes, always a feature of life in agrarian India, has grown into one of the most important fissures in the politics of North India in the past two decades. Thus, the Hindu majority is demonstrably a project, not a fact, and like all racialized categories and all predatory identities, it requires mobilization through the discourses of crisis and the practices of violence. The existence of minorities, such as Muslims, is an important aspect of these crises and practices, but the relation is not one of simple contrast and stereotyping, as I proposed earlier.

The relationship between Hindu caste politics and the anti-Muslim propaganda of the Hindu Right, especially since the 1980s, is also tied up with a major feature of Indian electoral politics since Indian independence, which is captured in the discourse of the vote bank. Indian elections are frequently seen, especially at the rural, local level, as turning substantially on the power of this or that party or candidate to capture a whole set of votes from a particular caste or religious community, which is bought off through its elites, and constitutes a vote bank. Bringing together the associations of an elite-manipulated, collectivized vote and of a vote bought corruptly, the image of the vote bank, which is freely used by all Indian politicians against one another, captures the deep history of links between the census and British colonial ideas of community and electorate, notoriously institutionalized in the separate electorates created early in the twentieth century for Hindus and Muslims in local elections under colonial rule. These enumerated communities (Kaviraj 1992) remain a major nightmare for liberal thought in India, because they catch the liberal abhorrence both of mass politics and its special corruptions and of the negative drag of ascription and kinship in a modernizing democracy. Today, the importance of vote banks has been somewhat undercut by the growing power of independent grassroots movements which resist wholesale manipulation by politicians as well as the cynicism with which politicians often make and break alliances and affiliations. Still, the Hindu Right never lost an opportunity to raise the specter of the Muslim vote bank, often accusing its major competitor, the now victorious Congress Party, of pandering to Muslims in an effort to capture the Muslim vote bank in local elections and, by implication, in state and national elections. The amazing defeat of the BJP in the 2004 general elections showed that this particular bogey was not enough to buy the loyalty of the largely rural Indian electorate.

This point brings us to the final feature of the fear of minorities in India, which has wider implications. The Hindu Right, especially through its dominant political parties, has consistently accused the Congress (the party historically associated with Nehruvian secularism, pluralism, and active tolerance of Muslims as a cultural minority) of appeasement in its dealings with Muslims' demands, complaints, and claims on the state. The discourse of appeasement is fascinating, because it is deeply linked to the slippage I earlier discussed between the sense of being a majority and the frustration of incomplete identification with the undivided ethnos of the polity. When the Hindu Right baits secular parties and movements with the charge of "appeasing" Muslims, it implies both a certain opportunism and cowardice on the part of the secularists and simultaneously (as with the Nazis and Munich) creates an image of the slippery slope which leads from the fear of giving in to this or that local demand of Muslim communities to giving in wholesale in the militarized, now nuclearized battle with Pakistan, which is the large-scale backdrop of all militant Hindu propaganda in India. The discourse of appeasement is the link between minority claims within national boundaries and the struggle with enemy states across the border, in this case Pakistan.

Thus, appeasement is another discursive device that allows the small numbers of Indian Muslims to be swollen and impregnated with the threat of Pakistan and, beyond that, of the militant multitudes of the world of global Islam. In the period immediately following the 9/11 attacks, as I have argued above in this chapter, these connections were revived and reimagined through the global invocation of Islamic terrorism. I turn now, by way of conclusion, to the figure of the suicide bomber, born in the struggles between Tamils and Sinhalas in Sri Lanka in the 1970s, and the relationship of this solitary figure to issues of number, minority, and terror.

How Small Are Small Numbers?
Minorities, Diasporas, and Terror

The suicide bomber, whether in Israel, Sri Lanka, New York, Iraq, or London, is the darkest possible version of the liberal value placed on the individual, the number "one." The suicide bomber today is the ideal type of the terrorist, since in this figure several nightmares are condensed. He or she, first of all, completely closes the boundary between the body and the weapon of terror. Whether by strapping bombs to his or her body or by otherwise disguising explosives in his or her body, the suicide bomber is an explosive body that promises to distribute its own bloody fragments and mix them in with the bloody parts of the civilian populations it is intended to decimate. Thus, not only does the suicide bomber elude detection, he or she also produces a horrible mixture of blood and body between enemies, thus violating not only the soil of the nation but the very bodies of the victims, infecting them with the blood of the martyr. Second, the suicide bomber is a revolting version of the idea of the martyr, highly valued in Christianity and Islam, for instead of being a passive martyr, he or she is an active, dangerous, exploding martyr, a murderous martyr. Third, the suicide bomber, as with the brainwashed agent in *The Manchurian Candidate*, is invariably portrayed as being in some paranormal state of conviction, ecstasy, and purpose, often built up through quasi-religious techniques such as isolation, indoctrination, and drug-induced hallucination, on the eve of the suicidal attack. This image is the very antithesis of the liberal individual acting in her interest, for the idea of a willingly exploded body does not fit easily into most models of rational choice. Fourth, imagined as an automaton, the suicide bomber, while a terrifying example of the individual, the number "one," is in fact always seen as an instance of the crazed mob or mass, the victim of propaganda and extrarational conviction, a perfect example of the mindless regimentation of the masses and of the dangerous unpredictability of the mob.

In all these regards, the suicide bomber is the pure and most abstract form of the terrorist. In this sense, the suicide bomber also captures some of the central fears surrounding terror. As a figure that has to get close to the place of attack by appearing to be a normal citizen, the suicide bomber takes to the extreme the problem of uncertainty which I have discussed earlier. In one suicide bombing in Israel, a suicide bomber disguised himself as a rabbi, thus subverting the very heart of the visible moral order of Israeli Jewish society. Likewise, the suicide bomber thrives in the spaces of civilian life, thus producing a form of permanent emergency that also requires a new approach to the problem of civilians and civil life in the age of globalized terrorism. This brings us to a final feature of the problem of small numbers in an era of globalized networks of terror, such as those that became a full part of public consciousness after 9/11.

Small Numbers and Global Networks

The events of 9/11 are now sufficiently behind us that we can begin to sift through the xenophobia, sentimentality, and shock that the attacks produced to ponder the more persistent images that remain from that event, now to be seen via the dark glass of the war on Iraq. Osama bin Laden is almost certainly alive, the Taliban are regrouping in Afghanistan and Pakistan, various warlords keep Afghanistan in a profound state of dependency on foreign money, arms, and soldiers, and there is a fierce insurgency against American forces in Iraq. The Iraqis, subdued initially by shock and awe, seem to hate Americans as much as they did Saddam Hussein, and the weapons of mass destruction seem to be alibis for the weapons of mass construction, largely in the hands of Bechtel and Halliburton. In both Afghanistan and Iraq, most especially in Iraq, the United States appears to be experimenting with a new political form, which may be called "long-distance democracy," a strange form of imperial federalism, where Iraq is treated as just another American state, operating under the jurisdiction of the National Guard and various other Federal forces from Washington in order to handle a disaster (produced in this instance by the decapitation of Saddam's regime).

The problem of numbers, minorities, and terror is alive and well in Iraq, along with the question of whether an Iraqi "people" can be produced out of the chaotic megapolitics of Shias, Kurds, and other large minorities. On one hand, the U.S. administration in Iraq faces the bewildering problem of minorities, such as the Shias, who are in absolute numerical terms very large and well connected to the ruling regime of Iran, or the Kurds, who span the borders of Iran, Iraq, and Turkey and constitute a huge minority. As the United States completes its nonexit, having rushed in teams of experts to build an Iraqi constitution overnight (just as they did in Afghanistan), there is a deep conceptual logjam involving large numerical minorities, the insistence among most Iraqis that the new polity has to be "Islamic," and the sense that a real democracy cannot be Islamic, except in the thinnest sense. Struggles over the nature of such basic ideas as constitutionalism, election, democracy, and representation go on in Iraq in the shadow of tank battles and full-scale warfare in places like Najaf and Falluja.

Two points about the ongoing Iraq debacle are relevant to the problem of small numbers and the fear of minorities. One is that even after ending the career of a truly murderous despot, likely feared and hated by many Iraqis, the U.S. military is still dogged by the fear of small numbers, those small groups of militia, civilians, and others who conduct sneak attacks on the U.S. forces and sometimes take suicidal risks to inflict damage and kill U.S. soldiers. Fully embedded as they are within the civilian population, finding these "terrorists" is a nightmarish task of divination for U.S. forces that counted on total Iraqi surrender after one evil individual—Saddam Hussein—had been toppled from power. Thus the United States, as an occupying power in Iraq, faces the fear that the small numbers who are continuing to torment and kill its soldiers are true representatives of the Iraqi people, who were originally scripted to greet the Americans as liberators and unfold the spectacle of a civil society underneath the carcass of the dictator.

Iraq also represents the more abstract challenge of producing a national people from what seem to be only large ethnic or religious minorities. In both Iraq and Afghanistan, the United States found itself between a rock and a hard place as it embarked on the project of building long-distance democracies: either they must allow these countries to constitute themselves as Islamic republics, thus recognizing that the only way to create peoples is by placing the very religion they most fear at the heart of the definition of the nation, or they must find ways to assemble coalitions of numerically large minorities, thus conceding that civil society in Iraq and in many places like Iraq has to be built over a long period of time, and that all there is to work with are minorities. But these are minorities with global connections and large populations associated with them. In facing this difficult set of choices, after starting a war that refuses to end, the United States has to engage with issues of minority, uncertainty, terror, and ethnic violence that plague many societies in the era of globalization. There are indications that some Iraqis may already be engaged in what has been called ethnic dry-cleaning in preparation for more brutal ethnic cleansing. If that scenario comes to pass, we will need, more than ever, to find new ways of negotiating the distance between groups of small numbers that provoke rage in the world's mobilized majorities, whose large numbers Lenin presciently saw as marking the beginnings of what he considered "serious politics."

Globalization, Numbers, Difference

I now return to two important themes: one is the issue of minor differences and the other is the special link between globalization and the growing rage against minorities. In my view, these themes are not unrelated. Michael Ignatieff (1998) is perhaps the most articulate analyst to invoke Freud's famous essay on "the narcissism of minor differences" in order to deepen our sense of the ethnic battles of the 1990s, especially in Eastern Europe. Mostly informed by his deep knowledge of that region, Ignatieff uses Freud's insight about the psychodynamics of narcissism to cast light on why groups like the Serbs and the Croats should come to invest so much in mutual hatred, given the complex interweaving of their histories, languages, and identities over many centuries. This is a fruitful observation that can be extended and deepened by reference to some of the arguments developed here.

In particular, I suggested that it was the small gap between majority status and complete or total national ethnic purity that could be the source of the extreme rage against targeted ethnic others. This suggestion — what I earlier glossed as the anxiety of incompleteness — allows us a further basis for extending Freud's insight into complex, large-scale, public forms of violence, since it allows us to see how narcissistic wounds, at the level of public ideologies about group identity, can be turned outward and become incitements to the formation of what I have called "predatory identities." The underlying dynamic here is the inner reciprocity between the categories of majority and minority. As abstractions produced by census techniques and liberal proceduralism, majorities can always be mobilized to think that they are in danger of becoming *minor* (culturally or numerically) and to fear that minorities, conversely, can easily become *major* (through brute accelerated reproduction or subtler legal or political means). These linked fears are a peculiarly modern product of the inner reciprocity of these categories, which also sets the conditions for the fear that they might morph into one another.

And this is also where globalization comes in. In a variety of ways, globalization intensifies the possibility of this volatile morphing, so that the naturalness that all group identities seek and assume is perennially threatened by the abstract affinity of the very categories of majority and minority. Global migrations across and within national boundaries constantly unsettle the glue that attaches persons to ideologies of soil and territory. The global flow of mass-mediated, sometimes commoditized, images of self and other create a growing archive of hybridities that unsettle the hard lines at the edges of large-scale identities. Modern states frequently manipulate and alter the nature of the categories through which they conduct their censuses and the statistical means through which they enumerate the populations within these groups. The global spread of improvised ideologies of constitutionalism, with elements drawn from the United States, France, and England, provokes new globalized debates about ethnicity, minority, and electoral legitimacy, as we see today in Iraq. Finally, the multiple, rapid, and largely invisible ways in which large-scale funds move through official interstate channels, quasi-legal commercial channels, and completely illicit channels tied up with networks like Al-Qaeda are intimately tied up with globalized institutions for money laundering, electronic transfers, and new forms of cross-border accounting and law, all of which constitute that form of finance capital which virtually defines the era of globalization. These rapid, often invisible, and frequently illicit movements of money across national boundaries are widely, and rightly, seen as creating the means for today's minority to become tomorrow's majority. Each of these factors can contribute to the exacerbation of social uncertainty—the subject of detailed analysis throughout this book—and thus create the conditions for crossing the line from majoritarian anxiety to full-scale predation, even to genocide.

Thus, the fear of small numbers is intimately tied up with the tensions produced for liberal social theory and its institutions by the forces of globalization. Minorities in a globalizing world are a constant reminder of the incompleteness of national purity. And when the conditions—notably those surrounding social uncertainty—within any particular national polity are ripe for this incompleteness to be mobilized as a volatile deficit, the rage of genocide can be produced, especially in those liberal polities where the idea of minority has, in some way, come to be a shared political value affecting all numbers, large and small.

Note

1. I owe this important point to Faisal Devji, who made it in the context of a lecture on the partition of British India at Yale University in fall 2003.

5 Our Terrorists, Ourselves

E arlier, I proposed that there is both mutual dependence as well as fierce struggle between vertebrate and cellular systems for the large-scale coordination of persons, resources, and loyalties. Contemporary terrorism, that is, violent action against public spaces and civilian populations in the name of antistate politics, is surely based on a cellular form of global organization, and one which has been forced into our consciousness by the 9/11 attacks. I have also suggested that this tectonic struggle surrounds and symptomatizes the current crisis of the system of nation-states. Here, I propose to look more closely at events in South Asia after 9/11, since in this region we seem to have a fractal ripple of the events of 9/11 and the attacks by the United States first on Afghanistan and then on Iraq. This fractal ripple appears to reproduce uncannily the battle between terrorists and states, between cellular and vertebrate forms of violence, and between struggles for local political identity and the realist diplomacy of established states. In this fractal movement,

Israel-Palestine is a mediating term, which allows the politics of New York City to meld into the politics of Kashmir. These events are both ripples and replications. Among the many questions they raise is the meaning of terror from a domestic point of view.

Terror and Uncertainty

Successful terrorist actions such as those of 9/11 return us to the problem of social uncertainty, a central concern of this study. First of all, the uncertainty has to do with the agents of such violence. Who are they? What faces are behind the masks? What names do they use? Who arms and supports them? How many of them are there? Where are they hidden? What do they want?

Elsewhere when discussing the relationship between uncertainty and large-scale ethnic violence in the 1990s, I suggested that such violence could be viewed as a complex response to intolerable levels of uncertainty about group identities (1998b). In that argument, large-scale exercises in counting and naming populations in the modern period and worries about peoplehood, entitlements, and geographical mobility created situations where large numbers of people turned immoderately suspicious about the "real" identities of their ethnic neighbors. That is, they begin to suspect that the everyday contrastive labels with which they live (in what I have called benign relations) conceal dangerous collective identities which can be handled only by ethnocide or some form of extreme social death for the ethnic other. In this case, one or both paired identities begin to seem predatory to one another. That is, one group begins to feel that the very existence of the other group is a danger to its own survival. State propaganda, economic fear, and migratory turbulence feed directly into this shift, and it frequently moves along the road to ethnocide. In Africa, for example, it is directly linked to movements for what is called "autochthony," which involves primary claims to peoplehood, territory, and citizenship for persons who can show that they are *from* their respective places, unlike others who are migrants or foreigners. In societies in which all regions have been produced by long-term and large-scale migrations, this is obviously a deadly distinction. And because it is hard to make, large-scale bodily violence becomes a forensic means for establishing sharp lines between normally mixed identities.

Bodily violence in the name of ethnicity becomes the vivisectionist tool to establish the reality behind the mask. And of course such violence invariably confirms its conjecture, for the dead, disabled, or deconstructed body of the suspect always confirms the suspicion of its treachery. Much of the best ethnographic literature on mass ethnic violence, even going back to the Nazi period, is full of the language of masks, treachery, betrayal, and exposure. Violence is part of the deadly epistemology of ethnocide. Of course, such violence breeds counterviolence, which takes on similar vivisectionist forms. In the masked violence of Belfast, Nablus, the Basque Country, and Kashmir, to name just a few examples, the mask of the armed terrorist actually reflects and confirms the suspicion of many dominant ethnic groups. When terrorists wear masks, and even when they do not wear masks, their ordinary demeanors are seen as organic masks for their real identities, their violent intentions, their treasonous loyalties, their secret betrayals. So every time an official police force rips off the mask of a dead or captured terrorist, what they reveal beneath the mask is another mask, that of an ordinary Muslim, or Palestinian, or Afghan, or Chechen, a traitor by definition.

Thus, the extreme bodily violence between ethnic groups, especially against ethnic minorities, which we have witnessed throughout the world in the 1990s, is not just testimony to our perennial bestiality or evolutionary tendency to wipe out the "them" to reassure the survival of the "us." Nor is it just the same as all the religious and ethnic violence over the centuries. The brutal ethnic violence of the 1990s is deeply inflected by factors which triangulate a highly specific sort of modernity: passport-based national identities; census-based ideas of majority and minority; media-driven images of self and other; constitutions which conflate citizenship and ethnicity; and, most recently, ideas about democracy and the free market which have produced severe new struggles over enfranchisement and entitlement in many societies. These and other factors demand that we do not look at the large-scale group violence of the past few decades as a mere chapter in the story of human tendencies toward religious war or ethnocide.

Most important about these new forms of vivisectionist violence is their peculiar mobilization of social uncertainty and ideological certainty. State propaganda and fundamentalist ideologies of many kinds spread vicious certainties about the ethnic other—about its physical features, its plans, its methods, its duplicities, and the need for its extinction. The infamous "Protocol of the Elders of Zion" is perhaps the classical model of such a propaganda text. But no amount of politically induced panic and doctrinally induced conviction will move ordinary people to the sort of extreme violence against large groups of friends and neighbors that we read about in detail regarding Rwanda in the early 1990s. For such extreme violence against neighbors and friends to occur, a deep sort of social uncertainty must mix with high levels of doctrinal certainty. The worry this produces is that the ordinary faces of everyday life (with names, practices, and faiths different from one's own) are in fact masks of everydayness behind which lurk the real identities not of ethnic others but of traitors to the nation conceived as an ethnos. This is the lethal mix that produces the logic of ethnic purification. And of course such uncertainty is also socially induced and politically stimulated. It, too, partly comes from propaganda. But it also comes from other sources, often much closer to the locality and to the minor wounds of daily life, in which ethnically different groups cumulate little doubts, small grudges, and humble suspicions. With the arrival of larger scripts, of both certainty and uncertainty, these little stories feed into a narrative with an ethnocidal momentum. Rumors feed such momentum, but only insofar as they are framed by larger narratives. And such narratives typically come from states or from large-scale, well-organized political forces. Such forces can never produce the contingent conditions for the reception of their narratives (and here is the flaw of many propaganda theories), but without them many sparks would die quietly, long before they become fires.

What does social uncertainty have to do with terrorism? The link is that terrorism works through the tools of uncertainty. And this uncertainty comes in many forms. First of all, when terrorists attack and escape, we do not know exactly who they are. Sometimes, we do not know what they want or who exactly they wish to attack or kill. When they are especially bold, even suicidal, their motives mystify us, producing further uncertainty. They also provoke a deeper uncertainty about what may happen next. Terror is first of all the terror of the next attack. There is also the question of what boundaries terrorists respect. Terrorists blur the line between military and civilian space and create uncertainty about the very boundaries within which we take civil society to be sovereign. Terror is a kind of metastasis of war, war without spatial or temporal bounds. Terror divorces war from the idea of the nation. It opens the possibility that anyone may be a soldier in disguise, a sleeper among us, waiting to strike at the heart of our social slumber. The terrorist combines the qualities of the soldier and the spy, thus blurring another boundary on which modern politics has largely been based. This is an important dimension of what happened in South Asia after 9/11.

The Geography of Anger

India and Pakistan—and much of South Asia as a whole— were directly affected by the events of 9/11 and by the war on terror launched in Afghanistan in 2001 and extended to

Iraq shortly thereafter. Afghanistan and Iraq are intricately linked to the regional world in which Pakistan survives. And Pakistan and India, of course, have been locked in a permanent state of conflict since 1947, focused particularly on their struggles over Kashmir. After 9/11, both India and Pakistan were forced into a contest to ally themselves with the United States in the global war against terror. Pakistan became a crucial asset to the United States—placing its own national sovereignty in peril—by permitting the United States to use it as a military base in its battle against the Taliban and their ally, Osama bin Laden. India used the language of terror to describe Pakistan's own military interventions in Kashmir and Pakistan's sponsorship of internal terrorist actions in India. Thus South Asia in the months following 9/11 offers us a special opportunity to examine the geography of anger and to get some sense of the ways in which global, regional, national, and local spaces enter into relationships of replication and repercussion. This geography is one way to examine how the fear of small numbers and their *power* shape the mutual relationships of different spatial scales and sites. More simply, looking at India and Mumbai in the period following 9/11 lets us see how the language of terror produces a new political geography.

In India, this was the period in which the Hindu Right had achieved electoral dominance nationally at the end of almost two decades of careful efforts to erode the culture of secularism and the credibility of pluralist forces in India. The 9/11 attacks were golden opportunities for the ruling party, the Bharatiya Janata Party (BJP) and its allies on the Hindu

Right, to bring together a number of their agendas. These included a long-standing interest in conflating India's Muslims with those of Pakistan; a strong program to strengthen India's armed (including nuclear) capabilities and to prepare Indians for the prospect of a final and decisive war with Pakistan; a domestic campaign to wipe out special treatment for all non-Hindu groups, especially Muslims, notably in areas of the personal law; and a systematic effort to rewrite Indian national history (and children's textbooks, among other texts) to reflect their view of India as a Hindu civilization which had been violated by Muslim invaders in the pre-British period and was endangered by Pakistan today.

The BJP, along with many other Hindu nationalist groups and organizations, has been at the heart of the national campaign which led to the physical destruction of the Babri Masjid, a major Muslim mosque in the north India pilgrimage center of Ayodhya, associated with the Hindu god-hero, Rama, in December 1992. Throughout the 1980s, the BJP had put great energy into rewriting the geography of India as Hindu geography, with major Muslim shrines portrayed as illegitimate structures built on sacred Hindu sites and shrines. This Hindu geography was combined with a paranoid nationalist geography, in which Pakistan was treated as an abomination, and war with Pakistan was discussed simultaneously as a project both of security and of purity. In this manner the BJP made a national effort to mobilize sentiment against Muslim rights within India, the Muslim state of Pakistan, and the Islamic presence throughout the world. After 9/11, this effort was enriched by the infusion of language taken from the global war on terror, which, for the BJP and its allies, became one and the same as the national campaign to reduce Muslims to a humiliated and ghettoized minority. This campaign was more than a small part of the ethnocidal rage against Muslims that the BJP managed to harness and coordinate in the pogroms against Muslims in February and March 2002, after a small group of Muslim youth set fire to a train compartment filled with Hindu activists returning from the sacred shrine at Ayodhya. The BJP lost the national general elections in 2004 but remains entrenched in Indian politics and is still the ruling elected party in the state of Gujarat.

We shall return to the Gujarat anti-Muslim pogroms shortly. But let us note that within India the months following 9/11 also saw the transformation of various local and regional geographies into parts of the larger geography of national outrage and global rage against terror. Consider the city of Mumbai, the capital of the state of Maharashtra, which has a long history of Hindu-Muslim riots but also a long history of traffic and commerce between Hindus and Muslims in sport, business, the film industry, and the retail world, among other aspects of life.

In Mumbai, Indian politics has its own specific ways of playing itself out, as it does in other states and regions. In that great commercial city, the story of national purity and military preparedness is, as always, somewhat overshadowed by news of Bollywood or cricket. This is the city of productions in living cash and color. Word of the death of Harshad "Big Bull" Mehta, a fraudulent investment banker; the doings of the first family of Indian cinema, the Bachchans; and the re-activation of the criminal proceedings against the mega film producer and diamond merchant, Bharat Shah, accused of links to the mafia, all remind one that in Mumbai all else bows to the nervous system of cash, wealth, glamour, and style.

Yet, Mumbai after 9/11 had its own ways of registering the anxiety about Pakistan and the nervousness about its own large Muslim populations. There was increasing scrutiny by the police of slum populations, especially those living in or near important military or transportation facilities. The arrest of Afroz Khan, resident of one of Mumbai's oldest slums, Cheeta Camp, with links to the worldwide terrorist attacks on New York City, Delhi, Sydney, and elsewhere firmly placed Mumbai and its police in the worldwide hunt for terrorists. In Mumbai, the subtext that links Muslims, slums, and "nests" for terrorists is particularly articulate; and frontier towns like Mumbra, where municipal and police writs are limited, were targeted by police and the media as natural escape hatches and secure zones for terrorists, especially terrorists with links to the groups alleged to be based in and supported by Pakistan. One action that linked housing (perhaps Mumbai's most desperate everyday issue) to terrorism was the amazing decree by the then Commissioner of Police in Mumbai, M. N. Singh, that all landlords must report the names and details of all new tenants, subtenants, or residents in the buildings they control. This amazing panoptical exercise was sure to fail in a city of twelve to fifteen million people (and is now largely forgotten), but it could certainly have provided an additional tool for police invasion of privacy in predominantly Muslim areas.

There is in all this more than a shade of the events of 1992 when the Babri Masjid in Ayodhya was destroyed by Hindu fundamentalists, leading up to the deadly riots of December 1992 and January 1993 and the bomb blasts later that year (which were widely seen as reprisals by Muslim groups with support from Mumbai's underworld).

The relationship between national security and anxieties about terrorism and crime is always, in Mumbai, linked to certain extraterritorial images of places like Dubai, Karachi, and increasingly Kathmandu, Bangkok, and Manila. With Dubai as the main one among these, there is a complex web of narratives involving major Mumbai-grown criminals now working out of Karachi and Dubai, links with Inter-Services Intelligence in Pakistan, bases in the countries that surround India, and active criminal partners and representatives in Mumbai (and elsewhere in India) who do the bidding of these all-powerful figures. Thus, in Mumbai, state discourse about terrorism, mainly articulated by the police, is always interconnected with older narratives about the underworld and the film world, smuggling, and the growing number of "encounters" between police and gangsters which amount to armed warfare in Mumbai's most crowded areas on virtually a daily or weekly basis. Yet another strand that refracts the Mumbai experience of these national and regional themes is the campaigns against hawkers, part of a long-standing struggle between the state and certain middle-class interest groups on one hand and poorer street hawkers on the other. Zealous municipal officials have waged a war against street vendors. These battles too have a strong communal subtext, since many of these hawkers happen to be Muslim and connected to Muslim elements in Mumbai's underworld and to other forms of muscle and protection. The war against hawkers is a struggle about space, civility, encroachment, and public order in Mumbai. But it too is not separate from the subtexts of crime, legality, security, and order.

The Shiva Sena, the right-wing nativist party that has the longest record of organizing anti-Muslim sentiments and activities in Mumbai, is and always has been the clearest voice in the effort to link civic issues to anti-Muslim provocations. In recent years, in an amazing act of political nerve, the Sena has organized a series of *maha-arati*[1] performances in a large number of temples and public spaces in Mumbai on the argument that these were ritual occasions for bringing "peace" to Mumbai and to the world. The outrageous feature of these claims is that it is exactly these large-scale rituals which, in 1992–93, were the main instrument for organizing anti-Muslim mobs, for making inflammatory speeches, and for linking Hindu megarituals with the direct intimidation of Muslim communities and neighborhoods. To restore these rituals in the period after 9/11 was in one stroke to restore the deadly propaganda links between Muslims and Pakistan, while casting Hinduism in the role of a peacemaking force.

Finally, in a fairly steady development of the past decade, the Indian navy has become a visible state and ritual presence in Mumbai. Always the key player in Mumbai's defenses, the Indian navy has staged a series of spectacular pageants of oceanic might off Mumbai's shores in recent years, hosting friendly navies, displaying its newest military wares, and anticipating its critical role in any future confrontation with Pakistan. Thus Mumbai's shores, previewed as a potential landing zone for Pakistani submarines in 1992–93, are now decisively seen as part of India's armed borders, its Line of Control, and Mumbai is increasingly inscribed into India's frontline by the navy and the media, more than ever in the past. The Arabian Sea is increasingly part of the Indian Ocean as a strategic zone, and the oceanic distance between Karachi and Mumbai is never far from its public imagination. Distances are always partly a matter of feeling and sensibility, and the Indian navy has done a fine job of shrinking the marine distance between India and Pakistan. And what the navy does on the coasts and in the harbors of Mumbai, the Shiva Sena and the police (though not always in harmony) do in the buildings, neighborhoods, and streets of Mumbai. The joint effect of these practices is to create a gradually superimposed mental map, in which war, security, crime, and terror overlay the geography of commerce, transport, work, and consumption.

This brief discussion has sought to provide one example of the ways in which events and spaces were recombined by the narratives of terror after 9/11. National politics, global alliances, regional tensions between states—all come into new relations which exemplify the ways in which the geography of anger is formed. Such geographies were produced and transformed throughout the world after 9/11. In every case, they brought together long-standing regional and local histories, national and transnational political tensions, and global and international pressures and coalitions. We have looked closely at India, at Maharashtra, and at the city of Mumbai. But we could do the same with many places, such as Kabul, Cairo, New York, and most recently, London, to which I turn shortly.

In every case, the geography of anger is not a simple map of action and reaction, minoritization and resistance, nested hierarchies of space and site, neat sequences of cause and effect.[2] Rather, these geographies are the spatial outcome of complex interactions between faraway events and proximate fears, between old histories and new provocations, between rewritten borders and unwritten orders. The fuel of these geographies is certainly mass mediated (by the news media, by the Internet, by political speeches and messages, by incendiary reports and documents), but its sparks are the uncertainty about the enemy within and the anxiety about the always incomplete project of national purity. The geography of anger is produced in the volatile relationship between the maps of national and global politics (largely produced by official institutions and procedures) and the maps of sacred national space (produced by political and religious parties and movements).

This discussion of the geography of anger is intended to support two arguments. The first is that in a world characterized by global articulations and tensions between cellular and vertebrate political forms, regions, nations, and cities can produce complex fractal replicas of larger struggles. Thus, the tensions between India and Pakistan appear in mutant forms at various levels and scales: the global, the national, the regional, and the urban. In all of these the figures of the terrorist, the pure nation, the masked traitor, and the hidden enemy play a crucial role. But the exact shape of these common characters and the precise plots they animate are not replicas but fractals of wider perspectives and images. The second argument that these vignettes allow is that there is now a freshly charged relationship between uncertainty in ordinary life and insecurity in the affairs of states.

There are many factors which affect the forms in which global dramas of war, peace, and terror arrive at different national and regional locations in different guises and take on highly specific synaptic connections to local anxieties and images of the "global." Among these factors, vital is the question of the media, its strength, its mix, its source of control, and its global reach. The media—print as well as electronic—are major opinion makers throughout the world, as we all know. But we all also know that even at the highest levels of global control and circulation no one quite rules the roost. The remarkable rise of the Arabic-language global network, Al-Jazeera, as a competitor to CNN and BBC, is perhaps the decisive case, which shows that the battle for global information and opinion is hardly over. And the same holds true at the level of smaller circles of mediation and circulation, where newspapers, magazines, cable stations, films, and political speeches provide highly variable paths through which news and opinion can filter and reverberate. In India, for example, the struggles among a variety of television conglomerates, Indian and multinational; the power of the information and broadcasting ministry; the ability of cable operators to hijack and pirate all sorts of media commodities and control their local distribution; the huge multilanguage press which modifies received Western and English opinion; and the direct access of many Indians to overseas news through work, kinship, and commercial ties create a very complicated circulatory system for the formation of public opinion and for the mediation of fear, panic, and the sense of emergency. To this mix may be added the new catalyst of Internet-based news and opinion flow, which allows a large variety of interest groups to disseminate their views and news and to select constituencies without regard to national boundaries.

And there is of course the global economy — globalization proper — that regime of open markets, increased integration of economies, and high-speed circulation of speculative capital under which we have been living for at least three decades. As many have noted, there is no significant population now living outside the terms of this global economy, whose protocols, dynamics, and legalities are being constructed in key ways in the present. What is relevant about this larger process is the matter of the link between the losers in the regime of globalization and the anger that has inspired the sorts of attacks that we witnessed against major world powers before and since 9/11.

There is little doubt that the reservoir of what has properly been called hatred directed against the United States — the state — and America — the country — has complex roots and sources. Among them is the long record of American military violence during the past century, the arrogance of American foreign policy, and not least, the clear link between world capitalism, American wealth, the power of multinationals, and the policies of the Bretton-Woods institutions. Thomas Friedman, a prominent commentator in the pages of the *New*

York Times, not a Marxist by even the wildest stretch of the imagination, was most candid a few years ago in arguing that the United States must be the world's police officer (in such places as Kosovo) since it was the obvious engine as well as the greatest beneficiary of the global economic system (1999). Others may hedge on this point but it has more than a little truth to it. There is more to be said on the complex journey from U.S. global domination of an economy that is producing both more wealth and more losers at an alarming rate to a rapidly spreading culture of anti-Americanism. I address this in greater detail in chapter 6. But the links are there, even if they are subtle, varied, and sometimes subterranean.

We can return now to the complex new circuitry that links uncertainty in social life to insecurity within and between states. This new condition may be glossed as a worldwide state of insecurity which creates increasing numbers of what may be called *insecurity states*. Discussions of the relationship between security and insecurity have become increasingly rich among scholars in South Asia, as a recent collection edited by R. M. Basrur (2001) makes evident.[3]

In the realist world which we seem to have left behind us, the security concerns of states and the everyday uncertainties of citizens (or civilians in my own register) were relatively clearly set apart. The former had to do with war and peace, diplomacy and borders, defense budgets and world politics. The latter had to do with local law and order, social predictability and routine, reliable knowledge of the world of friends and neighbors, some sense of ownership of local space and local public spheres, some sense that tomorrow would, on the whole, be like today. Today, the insecurities of states and the uncertainties of civilian spaces and persons have become disturbingly intertwined, and terror, terrorism, and terrorists are where we can best see this new blurring.

This blurring is notably a two-way street, as we can clearly see in South Asia. Local factional struggles, elections, rumors, and conflicts become sources of everyday uncertainty, especially about the identity of one's neighbors and local fellow citizens. Ethnic identity is a special flash point for such uncertainty, but it can also take other somatic forms, involving language, clothing, gender, food, or race. When such uncertainty is written into wider processes of demographic change, economic fear, and population shifts, exacerbated by the excesses of mass mediation and state or quasi-state propaganda machines, as I suggested earlier, the mix of social certainty and uncertainty becomes volatile and metastatic violence can develop. Conversely, state insecurities can percolate down and through the capillaries of civil society through deliberate efforts at mass mobilization, the politicization of some or all of the armed forces, the selective imposition of policies of detention or repression, the ethnically targeted invigilation of particular communities, and legal discrimination against minorities, migrants, or other weak citizens. Such state insecurity is especially marked where states have lost clear links to mass politics, where ambiguous or selectively favorable economic policies are imposed on behalf of wider global interests or forces, and where states have begun to substitute fundamentally culturalist policies for developmentalist ones.

India is an especially interesting case in this regard because in previous policies of its BJP-led coalition there was a strange mix of free-market rhetoric (as in the creation of a ministry at the cabinet level for "disinvestment"), technological trendiness (as in the cult of information technology and the tech-driven nonresident Indian community), and cultural fundamentalism. The slogan here might be seen as "open markets—closed cultures." The ongoing tension between the official BJP leadership and the leadership of the Rashtriya Swayamsevak Sangh (National Volunteers Society) and the even more radical fringes of the Hindu Right lie particularly in the question of where economic and cultural sovereignties mix and meet. And even as the BJP increasingly rests its credibility on its stance on cultural heritage and historical correctness from a Hindu point of view, its politics has become steadily more hawkish, especially in the wake of the official nuclearization of India's armed forces. Since that time, and in the wake of India's triumph over Pakistan in Kargil a few years ago, there has been a steady effort by the BJP and its allies to equate modernity with technology (particularly information technology) and tradition with Hinduism and to claim to be the best guardian of both. The centerpiece of this dual approach includes a dramatic intensification of weapons building, including weapons related to nuclear power; an intransigent position on negotiation with anyone about Kashmir; and a steadfast commitment to linking Pakistani threats to external security with internal threats to Indian purity, especially from Islam but also from other "alien" religions. Thus, the cult of information and military technology goes side by side with an increasingly strident project to Hinduize Indian civil society at every level. It remains to be seen whether the ruling Congress Party, which won the general elections in 2004, can reverse these trends.

The actions of various cellular groups producing armed opposition to the Indian state in Kashmir, and now increasingly reaching across the border deep into Indian cities and facilities, opens a new opportunity for the state to penetrate civil society in the name of its own insecurities about borders, sabotage, and internal terrorism. This is not to deny that there are in fact cross-border interests at work in India, sometimes with deep commitments to violent action. But it is to suggest that such violence has greatly strengthened the hands of those who wish to push the metaphor of war ever deeper into the crevices of daily life. For many sectors of the Indian middle classes and for many sections of the urban and rural working classes, daily life has become indelibly colored by the sense of a cultural struggle which seamlessly links war and politics at the borders with vigilance and purification at the centers. From Wagah to Ayodhya[4] is but a shift of theaters of war, and here there is a link between Pakistan, its terrorists, Indian Muslims, and their implicit treachery. The successful effort by the police in Mumbai to stop the staging of a Marathi language play about Nathuram Godse (the Hindu killer of Mahatma Gandhi) in 2002 was without a doubt underwritten by the public sense that India is a country (almost) at war with Pakistan. Such state actions feed into the uncertainties of everyday life, and in a given week or month in a place like Mumbai intercut themselves with newspaper stories about Muslim terrorists living in princely dwellings in slum areas (allegedly funded by Al-Qaeda or similar networks) and by more general calls to "clean" out slums especially dominated by Muslims, which are alleged to be ideal havens for terrorists from Kashmir and beyond. Here again are the metaphors used by the Nazis in places such as Warsaw about hunting the vermin (as they described the Jews of Poland) and of various groups to describe poor Muslim areas in cities such as Delhi.

Indeed, state insecurity and social uncertainty about ethnicized others feed on each other in a disturbing spiral in the era of global terror. For once terrorism is shown to cross national boundaries (as it plainly does) and once it is shown to work by stealth and disguise, then this connection is easy to mark and mobilize. And going back to the trope of vivisection (which I used earlier), both state-sponsored violence against terrorists and local violence against ethnic neighbors converge on the display of the captured, wounded, or humiliated body of the enemy as the proof of the very treachery it was designed to destroy. In the repose of death or the immobility of surrender, terrorist bodies become silent memorials to the enemy within, proof of treachery in its very pathetic ordinariness.

Terror in the Capital of Capital

The United States of course is engaged in a new set of battles over state security and civil uncertainty after 9/11. And as in India, the attacks of 9/11 have unleashed a new order of convergence between everyday social uncertainties about us and them and the insecurities of an enraged megastate. As this Gulliver breaks the bonds of the many Lilliputians that have been plaguing it for some time and wreaks its havoc on Afghanistan and now Iraq, many parallel battles have been launched against illegal migrants, suspicious travelers, and dissent of every kind. New debates have been unleashed about the limits of state surveillance, about the need to protect minorities of color against hate crimes resulting directly from the events of 9/11, and about the constitutionality of military trials for those detained by state security forces immediately after the 9/11 attacks.

The problematic of terror in the public sphere in the United States has a very different logic from that in the South Asian region. Terror provokes new debates about immigration, which arguably has been the central policy dilemma of the United States in the past fifty years. It arouses new arguments about civil rights, especially the rights to privacy and freedom of movement. It has made it very difficult to mount a serious critique of the upscaling of defense expenditures across the board. And it raises the worst worry of all, the one few people want to think about, over the link between the attack on the Federal Building in Oklahoma city by Timothy McVeigh and his supporters and the attack on the World Trade Center in the early nineties and again on 9/11.

This last is the central point that links the refractions of terrorism in otherwise very different sites of the global economy. Whether in the United States or in India, terror organized by cellular networks terrifies the vertebrate structures of the state and blurs the lines between the enemies within and the enemies outside. Thus terrorists, everywhere in the world, cast a dark shadow on our own deepest anxieties about national identity, state power, and the ethnic purity that all nations somehow depend on. Our terrorists, whether in the United States, India, or elsewhere, are therefore doubly horrifying: they are malignant, to be sure, but they also somehow seem to be symptoms of the deep malaise in our own social and political bodies. They cannot easily be exorcised as evil spirits or simply amputated like bad limbs. They force a deeper engagement with our states, our world, and our selves.

Closing the Loop

We can now try to close the explanatory loop and bring together the fearful symmetry between the *power* of small numbers—the central feature of cellular terrorism and suicide bombing—and the *fear* of small numbers—the paradoxical weakness of liberal democracy in the era of globalization.

In July 2005, just a few weeks before this book was sent to press, London was shaken by a series of bomb blasts that shook the British nation. Producing death and mayhem in the Western capital city best prepared to deal with urban terrorism, the bombs have been traced to a group of young men linked largely by their status as nonnatives in a multicultural Britain, who may have come together in the context of England's large network of mosques, religious schools, and Islamic communities. Though there are variations within the group and many questions about how they came to be transformed into urban terrorists, it does seem clear that several of the bombers and their families were part of the Pakistani diaspora to England, and others have ties to the Indian state of Gujarat, which lies along the Indo-Pakistani border. What do these facts have to do with the larger arguments of this book about minority, uncertainty, globalization, and violence?

The bomb attacks of July 2005 in London allow us to bring the story of 9/11 into the present and take a closer look at the dynamics of terror and ethnocide by examining in some detail one particular strand of a larger global fabric. As we have seen in this chapter, Indian Muslims have been successfully portrayed by the Hindu Right as potential traitors to the

Indian nation, as secret agents for Pakistan on Indian soil, and as instruments of global Islam determined to undermine Hindu India. The state of Gujarat witnessed the most serious state-sponsored terror against its Muslim minority in February 2002, not long after the global war on terror was announced by the United States in the wake of the 9/11 attacks.

Although the BJP, the political party that sponsored this massive ethnocide in democratic India, was driven out of power in the national elections of 2004, the regional branch of this party remains in control of the state of Gujarat, and those BJP leaders who consciously moved Gujarat into a state of majoritarian rage are still very much in power in this important state. Gujarat is still a crucible for political hatred against Muslims and for state-sponsored fear of Pakistan.

Meanwhile, many young Muslims (among them many from both sides of the Pakistan-India border, including the state of Gujarat) have grown to adulthood as diasporic Britons in a multicultural world where they are by no means full citizens. Exposed to the messages of Islamic mullahs who believe in some form of permanent war against the West, unconvinced by the British mix of official multiculturalism and everyday racism, and aware of the attacks against ordinary Muslims throughout the liberal world, the psychology of liberal minorities dogs them in Britain and feeds on media and Internet reports of attacks on Muslims in Palestine, Kashmir, Gujarat, New York, and beyond. At the same time, the messages to which they are exposed from Muslim clerics in Britain and by other peers who have been radicalized is that they truly belong not to a terrorized minority but to a terrifying majority, the Muslim world itself.

In this process, in some instances, their self-perception as injured minorities gives way to a different sense of themselves as a vanguard minority who actually speak for a sacred majority — the Muslims of the world. This self-constructed minority is a very different sort of minority from those imagined by the British state. Born out of the shreds and patches of British multiculturalism, the new minorities out of which the London bombers emerged is indeed a minority to be feared, because it is the rogue voice of an injured global majority.

There are two ways to read this story. We can read it as one of the myriad ways in which a deep colonial history joins the dynamics of global minority politics. The partition of the Indian subcontinent is unimaginable without a series of institutional changes sponsored by the British in colonial India, ranging from religious counts in the nineteenth-century censuses, to separate electorates for Hindus and Muslims in the early twentieth century, to strategies for divide and rule that led directly to the creation of two nations in 1947. In turn, this colonial story sets the stage for one of the bloodiest political partitions in modern history, which puts India and Pakistan in a state of permanent antagonism for more than half a century. Some portion of this aggrieved population of Muslims from India and Pakistan ends up in Britain, land of the struggle over Salman Rushdie's *The Satanic Verses* in the late 1980s and Tony Blair's aggressive commitment to the cause of the United States in Iraq in 2003. On the Indian side, the wounds of Partition lead fairly directly to the rise of Hindu fundamentalism in Gujarat and a witch hunt and pogrom against its large Muslim community in 2004. Young Muslims (of Indian and Pakistani origin) in Britain could not have failed to make connections between 9/11 in New York, the war in Iraq and Afghanistan, the ongoing brutalization of their fellow Muslims in Palestine, the pogrom against Muslims in Gujarat in 2002, and the continued failure of the Indian state to punish the main perpetrators of the crimes against humanity committed there.

We can also read this story structurally and synchronically as a lesson in the slippery dynamics governing the status of minorities and majorities in many democratic societies in the last decade of the twentieth century. As some democratic nations incline to create internal minorities whom they perceive as external majorities in disguise, so some among these minorities—often educated, disaffected youth—begin to identify themselves with the cellular world of global terror rather than the isolating world of national minorities. Thus they morph from one kind of minority—weak, disempowered, disenfranchised, and angry — to another kind of minority — cellular, globalized, transnational, armed, and dangerous. This transformation is the crucible that produces recruits to global terrorism.

The history of Muslim minorities in the twenty-first century surely is the dominant tale of this kind of fearful symmetry between the fear of small numbers and the power of small numbers. But it is by no means unique. The world is full of angry minorities with the potential for cellular organization. We have already observed this capacity among militant Sikhs, Basques, Kurds, Tamil Sri Lankans, and other aggrieved minorities who have become diasporic global communities. So let us not suppose that there is something in the DNA of Islam that produces the capacity to morph compliant minorities into terrifying ones. With these observations about the relationship between violence against minorities and the violence of minorities, we are in a position to return to the world of ideological warfare in which we now live.

113

Notes

1. A *maha-arati* is a large, public prayer begun in recent years to showcase Hindu strength and solidarity.

2. In his brilliant recent book, *Landscapes of the Jihad* (2005), Faisal Devji makes two major arguments that further illuminate the geography of anger. The first is to show that the *jihadi* worldview is a complex historical outcome of the edge regions of the Islamic world rather than its core region. The second argument converges with my own ideas about ideocide and civicide by arguing that the violent vision of the *jihadis* is better seen as a

radical, alternative ethical universalism rather than a strictly anti-Western vision.

3. See especially the fine essay by Jayadeva Uyangoda whose use of the idea of insecurity converges interestingly with my own.

4. Wagah is a border post between India and Pakistan. Ayodhya is the city of the demolished Babri Mosque.

Samuel Huntington's argument (1993) about the clash of civilizations is fundamentally flawed. But it does have a certain intuitive appeal in the world we have entered after 9/11. By placing culture at its heart, the model appears to have presciently captured something of the sense of generalized war against the West, particularly the United States, that seems to have swept the Islamic world, and especially its terrorist extremes. So there is something right about this model and something wrong.

The part that is flawed, indeed fatally flawed, is its image of civilizations themselves, conceived in part racially, in part geographically, in part by religious affiliation, and in general as physical bastions of culture. This is primordialism with a macrogeographical base. It ignores the vast amount of global interaction between civilizational areas, it erases the dialogues and debates within geographical regions, and it deletes overlaps and hybridities. In a word, it evacuates history from culture, leaving only geography. The world appears as a large series of slowly moving cultural glaciers, with sharp contrasts at their boundaries and little variety within. This spatialization of culture, painted in large strokes in the trope of civilizations, also opens the door to a dangerous collapse of religion, culture, and race in Huntington's argument.

All this has been suggested in the many trenchant criticisms of this approach that have appeared since it was formulated by Huntington several years ago. But he was also right in a certain intuitive way. Right because he recognized that far from being at the "end of ideology," as Daniel Bell called it in the 1950s, or at "the end of history" as Francis Fukuyama put it several decades later, we seem to have entered a new phase of war in the name of ideology alone (Bell 1961; Fukuyama 1992). Huntingon's error was to conflate messenger and message and to map this complex reality into a realist geographical picture of actual, physical land masses which were seen as the homes of antagonistic civilizations. Especially in the case of Islam, this is a costly error because it feeds, perhaps unintentionally, the spatialized fantasies that led George Bush and his advisors to try to localize Al-Qaeda in Afghanistan and decimate a cell by erasing a landmass.

Yet even Bush and his associates recognized, from the very start, that there was something global, elusive, and nonspatialized—indeed virtual—about the new enemy. This quality is what I tried to capture in the distinction between vertebrate versus cellular organizations earlier. Huntington's model too, apart from its various other conceptual flaws, is a vertebrate model for a cellular world. But he was right to see that there was a new sort of ideological totalism afoot in the world, especially as regards the hatred of the United

States. This is where the idea of "ideocide" (which I also raised earlier in the book) comes in.

Ideocide and Civicide

Ideocide is a term that points to a widespread, indeed global, phenomenon, a new and serious phenomenon, whereby whole peoples, countries, and ways of life are regarded as noxious and outside the circle of humanity and as appropriate targets for what Orlando Patterson called "social death" (1982) in his discussion of slavery and what Daniel Goldhagen saw as the first step toward Nazi ethnocide and genocide regarding world Jewry (1996). This sentiment is too strong to be called a clash of civilizations. It can better be called a clash of *ideocides* or a clash of *civicides*. The politics in question is more than ethnocidal or even genocidal, since those terms have their anchors in the hatred of "internal" minorities. Ideocide or civicide turns this sentiment outward and targets whole ideologies, large regions, and ways of life as outside the pale of human ethical concern. Also, unlike earlier precursors such as Cold War Manichaeism, in which communism, for example, was seen as a total object of revulsion by Americans, the target in such cases is no longer specific states or political regimes but whole ideologies and ideas of civilization.

This part of my argument may seem like a simple restatement of Huntington's argument, but it is not. By shifting levels from clash to cleansing, we cross a crucial qualitative line, which also allows the shift from regimes as targets to whole populations as targets (the bin Laden slide, we may call it). Further, by focusing on ideas of civilization rather than civilizations as such, we recognize that such totalizing battles can occur *within* the great traditions and regions of the world and not just *across* them (the central flaw of the Huntington model). Thus, the huge and lengthy war between Iran and Iraq, now mostly forgotten in the Western media, is an example of a major battle between Shia and Sunni ideas of Islam, exacerbated by additional stimulations through the machinations of the two regimes after the ascension of Ayatollah Khomeini, to be sure. To cast real light on the new logics of ideocide and civicide, our best clue comes from the worldwide growth in the ethnic cleansing of minorities. Hitler was the first to link this internal issue (German Jews) to a total global project (the elimination of world Jewry). Elements of this globalizing of internal scapegoats can be seen in numerous examples in the past decade. Conversely, there is a growing tendency to see global moral enemies as being morally indistinguishable from local or internal enemies. This double logic—globalizing internal moral opponents and localizing faraway moral enemies—is the key to the logic of ideocide and civicide. It adds a powerful globalizing component to existing modalities of ethnocide and genocide.

Long-Distance Hatred

The second, difficult part of an alternative to the clash of civilizations model has to do with the United States and North American cultural life generally. There is no doubting the fact that in many different parts of the world and among various classes, religious groups, and intellectuals as well as among many ordinary people, a generalized hatred of the U.S. government, and of Americans as a people, is more widespread than we sometimes care to admit. This hatred needs to be understood. It has many roots and forms, not all confined to the Islamic world by any means. The first, which has been documented as long ago as the image of the ugly American, goes back to the everyday arrogance of Americans of every type in the world after 1945. As tourists, modernizers, World Bank officials, missionaries, researchers, do-gooders, and philanthropists, especially in the shadow of the battle with the Evil Empire, Americans in this period closed every gap between themselves, as people, and their government. Americans always seemed to be cultural ambassadors: in a way, every American who found himself or herself anywhere in the non-European world was seen as a walking bundle of American technological, military, cultural, and educational privilege, both flaunting their pleasures and restricting access to these pleasures. Every beggar who has stood outside the great hotels of the world, waiting for a large American couple to throw some kindness or some pennies at him or her, ever since 1945, is a small mujahideen in the making. And any American who has experienced the taunting of poor beggars anywhere in Asia, Africa, or the Middle East, knows that every act of supplication contains a hidden threat and a certain deep revulsion. Gunga Din is dead.

And there is a cultural dimension to this growing anti-Americanism. Offensive Germans and Japanese are not seen as ambassadors of their regimes, but Americans almost always are. Why is this so? The reason is that Americans embody, in their clothing, their style, their possessions, and their practices (such as jogging around their hotels in the third world) a special embodiment of the cultural machines that represent America on the television screens of the world: the beautiful bodies of *Baywatch*; the physical scale of the Schwarzeneggers and Stallones; the energy and vigor of *NYPD Blue*; the folksy humor of *I Love Lucy* and the caring aura of Oprah Winfrey (both of which are popular shows worldwide). In thus embodying the great cultural machineries of their society, ordinary Americans invoke the power and arrogance of the American state, since lifestyles have globally become the central sign of moral style. Moral styles, throughout the world, are now seen as dictated by state interests and restrictions. So, in an odd way, there is a growing tendency to link American bodies, American cultural glitz, and the known power of the American state. In the hands of those ideologues throughout the world who have made bodily morality central to state stability, Americans seem to symbolize the Nikes on their feet and in their missile silos simultaneously. Needless to say, most Americans who have lived, worked, or traveled in the poorer parts of the world would be horrified by this reading of what they might represent.

And in many parts of the world, this equation has been steadily consolidated by massive American military strikes against poorer countries (we can begin with Hiroshima and Nagasaki, move through Korea and Vietnam, and make a few side halts in Cuba, Chile, Panama, Iran, Iraq, and Afghanistan as well as Bangladesh, Somalia, and Haiti) and the undeniable Washington imprimatur on some of the most difficult policies imposed by the International Monetary Fund (IMF) and the World Bank.

The hardest pill to swallow is that most of the world appears to be desperate to come to the United States, to share its freedom and its entrepreneurial possibilities, to enjoy its goods and services, and to see the world from the cockpit rather than from the last seats in economy class. And this is really puzzling for most Americans. How can so many people hate us for the very things they desperately want and seek in trying to crash our borders, get our visas, and fly, drive, sail, or swim to our shores? Why expend huge energies getting to a land you despise? Why kill the very pleasures you hope to enjoy?

The clues to the answers to this question are not to be found in the devastation of Afghanistan after the war with the Soviets and by the anti-Marshall plan pursued by the United States once the Soviet Union left Afghanistan, nor are they to be found in the Palestinian refugee camps of Lebanon and elsewhere, nor are they even in those shadowy Pakistani madrassas where the Taliban are supposed to have been fired up and dumbed down, though all of these may be part of the background. They are to be found in talking to cabdrivers in many cities in the United States, people of modest means and lower-class backgrounds, frequently educated, mobile, and talented, who have chosen to enter the United States through the Statue of the Yellow Cab. Many of these cabdrivers (who come overwhelmingly from South Asia and Africa when they are not black Americans or Hispanics) are gung-ho Americans, celebrating their ability to work for themselves, be their own bosses, educate their children, or pursue their own educations in the United States. Every third cabdriver is checking out the Microsoft certification books and dreaming of cyber paradise. Others have more gritty goals: a few more cabs, a gas station, a convenience store perhaps.

But others speak with incredible contempt of Americans, of crime among blacks, of sexual looseness among whites, of immorality at every level, of the hypocrisy of police and city officials, of the everyday racism they experience. This moral contempt tells us something, and it is not about hypocrisy. These moral critics of everyday America, who see themselves as surviving in a moral cocoon within the belly of the beast, have found a way to separate American life (which they value and treasure) from the American "way of life," which in their versions of it they frequently abhor, especially in matters of sexual morality. This is not an easy separation to conceptualize, since it is part of a seamless web in everyday American cultural ideologies.

For the "wretched" of the world who come to make their lives in the United States, a curious split has emerged. As Americans, they have a powerful sense of their rights and freedoms, which they seek and enjoy to the fullest extent possible. As non-Americans, they retain the sense of revulsion, alienation, and distance that they may always have had. For such immigrants (legal or otherwise) civic patriotism has come asunder from political patriotism, in many cases. It is this gap they seek to cover up in the profusion of flags and other tokens they anxiously advertise in the streets of New York and beyond.

Another example comes from higher up the global class ladder. Most highly educated members of the Indian elite in my own age group (50–60) have family and friends in the United States and generally are enjoying high positions in medicine, technology, computers, banking, and finance. The younger among them are truly immigrant masters of this universe. They run companies, advise mayors and cabinets, run major journals and publishing houses, patent new bio and cyber technologies, and teach at most of the elite universities in the United States. In many cases, these privileged Indians have children now in elite colleges in the United States or hope to place them there, or they are helping to find them jobs after they graduate. This is the America they seek and pursue with unflagging vigor, networking, planning, and strategizing. And this is even truer of those members of the Indian elite who have elected to stay in India in their chosen professions. Yet, this is not hypocrisy either. How do we understand the fact that many of these elites in India and elsewhere love nothing more than to bash the United States (sometimes the government, sometimes the culture industries, sometimes just Americans as such) while pursuing their version of the American dream for themselves or for their children? These are enormously sophisticated people, among them stars of the corporate world and of the academy, articulate in English, media-savvy, slick in argument, forgiving in debate, self-effacing in combat. A far cry from the apologists of Osama. But how different are they? And why do they too bite the hand that feeds them?

The answer to this puzzle lies in another part of the process we call globalization. Most professional futures, whether in computers, mathematics, social science, or human rights, are made by standards produced and enforced in U.S. organizations, professional networks, and institutions. In other words, your success in virtually any nonstate career in the poorer parts of the world is likely to be measured by American-made standards or by Americans enforcing these standards.

This would not matter so much except that most poor countries and regions have destroyed their cities, weakened their academic institutions, made serious research and teaching impossible, and made many professional spaces colonies of the state, either through repression or through corruption. So, for these professionals and elites, there is a vast sucking noise, produced in the vacuums of their own professional worlds and anchored in America. So they pursue careers, their children's well-being, and their own professional networking in the United States (and to some extent elsewhere in the first world). At the same time, like the third-world cabdriver, they retain the right to be anti-American in matters of culture, politics, even lifestyle. They end up in America as civil immigrants but also as moral exiles. And even when they remain in their home countries, they retain this double relationship, which also provides fuel to the larger machinery of civicide in respect to the United States.

So, sadly, the dreamers and the haters are not two groups. They are often one and the same persons. And, in the case of the United States, because of its huge role as a world power since 1945 (and especially since 1989), this ambivalence is more dramatic. Thus, hatred for America is intimately tied up with the desire to be part of it. Spend a week outside any U.S. consulate seeking a visa to get in, filling a hundred forms, being pushed around in the queue, being insulted by petty local officials and then cross-examined by a tired visa officer and then turned down, and you will activate the hate gene too. The U.S. press regularly runs stories on these issues which are vivid testimonials to this little breeder reactor.

And there are many others who are ambivalent this way. Nongovernmental organization (NGO) activists who have to beg the World Bank for a few thousand dollars; doctors who fail the American Medical Association exams required to practice in the United States; students forced to return after their education because their job makers changed or vanished; managers in U.S.-controlled multinationals who find Americans (or Europeans) fifteen years younger than they controlling their regional headquarters; researchers who have struggled to get a single article published in a United States journal for decades finding themselves turned into native informants for American graduate students. Who needs the madrassas to breed hate?

For these professional elites, with cosmopolitan visions and aspirations, freedom and opportunity are not articles of cultural faith and icons of America, in the sense repeated endlessly by George Bush and his senior associates. Rather, freedom and opportunity are practical matters, associated with America as a civic rather than a political system. Again, in some sense what these outsiders seek is American society, not American polity. They seek opportunities as facts, not opportunity as a norm. Here is the slip, really the chasm, between official or indigenous patriotism and the more pragmatic desire for the good life that many would-be migrants to the United States seek. And here is where practical pleasure in life in the United States—or the aim to enter it—can be consistent with a deep moral resentment of American polity and the American government as global forces.

Sociologically speaking, two forces join to create the deep sources and channels of worldwide anti-American feeling. The ambivalence of global elites who resent the American disciplines that affect their lives and prospects, while occasionally excluding or degrading them, and the raw anger of the armies of the dispossessed, who imagine the United States through the lens of feudal lordship, of moral depravity, of direct bombings and remote control violence, and of economic disasters mediated through the World Bank and the IMF. The Islamic contribution to this mix, in the form of the redeployment of the concept of jihad against the United States—conceived as Satan in the world—adds a specific regional vector to this combustible mix. Other vectors exist elsewhere—in much of Latin America, where the United States is seen as an extension of the CIA and the large multinationals; in Japan, where the humiliations of World War II and the horrors of Hiroshima and Nagasaki are hardly forgotten; in India, where Hindu nationalists associate the United States with beauty pageants, rampant consumerism, and amoral hedonism; in much of Africa, where the United States is seen as the successor to the brutalities of European colonialism by some and as the hegemon of the world that is too busy to care about Africa. Such examples could be multiplied. They add specific regional and historical flavors to the mix of ambivalence from elites and deep fear and anger from the poorer masses.

We can now address the issue of long-distance hatred, which may be a distinctive contribution of the second half of the twentieth century, younger still than the short history of empathy at a distance, which Michael Ignatieff so eloquently discusses (1998). Ignatieff points out that even in the Christian West, it was not a natural thing to worry about the sufferings of those far away and that this capability for empathy at a distance is a special product of the liberal, humanist imagination which resists all suffering in the name of a felt and general humanity. But what about the baser emotions such as envy, hatred, and fear? How do they become plausible without face-to-face contact, direct resentment, local experiences? How do they become abstract and portable?

Here the recent history of internal ethnocide in places such as Yugoslavia, Rwanda, Indonesia, India, and Cambodia is only partly instructive, for these horrible cleansing campaigns involve distorted intimacies through which neighbors kill neighbors and familiars are turned into strangers and abominations. The Nazi success in thus turning German Jews into the "social dead" preceded their ability to mobilize campaigns to eliminate Jews in other parts of Europe and eventually in Russia.

But today's hatreds, such as the hatred of some Islamic thinkers, movements, and militants for Americans and the hatred of many Americans for Islamic peoples (conceived as Arabs, Muslims, or terrorists) is a more abstract hatred. For some, victims themselves of bombs, economic devastation, warfare, and abandonment (such as the Afghan mujahideen abandoned by the U.S. after the defeat of the Soviets in Afghanistan), hatred of the United States is indeed tied to intimate experiences of social suffering. But for many, it is a victory of the image and the message, of media and of propaganda. Media brings images of American prosperity, moral laxity, and global power through movies, television, and the Internet. Propaganda comes through local elites, who find in the United States a general theory and source of evil in the world. The question is: What makes these messages plausible, these images compelling? And how can they be incitements to hatred, to the impulse to what I have called civicide?

The move from garden variety resentment to generalized hatred of whole countries, populations, and societies, often hardly experienced concretely, requires us to understand the moral core of this hatred. The language of evil is rampant in the more extreme discourses of the Islamic world — and it has produced its self-fulfilling other in the images of devil, the evil, and the like used by the leaders of the United States. Long-distance hatred requires two lethal items to mix — a Manichaean theodicy that seeks to explain the moral rot in the world in one fell swoop and a set of images and messages in which this Manichaean theodicy can be anchored and made locally plausible. Long-distance hatred creates a moral image of complete evil and gives it the face of an entire society, people, or region. This is the fuel of ideocide and its policy consequence, civicide.

And civicide now thrives in a new post-Westphalian world. Surely the system of nation-states is not dead: some rise, some fall, all share the illusion of permanence. But the 9/11 attacks are a sure signal that the world of global politics, of diplomacy, warfare, resource flow, allegiance, and mobilization is only partly covered by the map of nation-states and the politics of international deals and flows. This Westphalian world may be described as real and realist, as resting on an architecture of mutuality and recognition in which nonstate actors were minor irritations, usually confined to domestic politics or, when they leaked across national boundaries, to be simple examples of criminality. Cross-border flows, in this older model, were either state sanctioned or criminal.

But, as I argued earlier, a new world has emerged as we move into the twenty-first century. We still have the vertebrate world, organized through the central spinal system of international balances of power, military treaties, economic alliances, and institutions of cooperation. But alongside this exists the cellular world, whose parts multiply by association and opportunity rather than by legislation or by design. It is also a product of globalization—of the new information technologies, of the speed of finance and the velocity of the news, of the movement of capital and the circulation of refugees. This emerging cellular world has two faces.

The dark face of this cellular politics has been my own preoccupation in this and in earlier chapters. It is the face we have come to call terrorism, where groups as diverse as the Irish Republican Army and the Red Brigades link up with like groups in the Middle East, Asia, and elsewhere to create large-scale violence in the heart of everyday life—in cafes, sporting events, financial centers, train and bus stations. These cellular organizations are sometimes a product of and are dependent on the nation-state, but they also have the potential to threaten the nation-state and not only by attacking this or that regime, in this region or that one. They threaten the system of nation-states by eroding its overall monopoly over the means of large-scale devastation of human life. By working outside the existing frameworks of sovereignty, territoriality, and national patriotism, they attack the moral framework of the nation-state as a global form and system.

This is the source of the real panic behind the pronouncements coming out of the civilian and military leadership in Washington and its allies. What if we are witnessing the birth of a new global system of power, politics, violence and its dissemination, completely outside the structure of the international system, not individual terrorist networks and cells, not even rogue states or alliances of rogue states, but a full-scale alternative global polity, with full access to lethal technologies of communication, planning, and devastation? And what if this alternative world system has as its principal object the means of violence now largely controlled through the state system?

These dark scenarios suggest an end not just to civil society but to the idea of civilian life itself. But long-distance politics, organized in new cellular forms, is not only the monopoly of rogue capitalists or political terrorists. It is also the organizational style of the most interesting progressive movements in global society, those movements which seek to construct a third space of circulation, independent of the spaces of state and market, and which we may call movements for grassroots globalization. I turn to a brief discussion of such movements as a way to conclude.

Grassroots Globalization

Cellular globalization does indeed have a more utopian face. The happier face is what has sometimes been called international civil society, those networks of activists concerned with human rights, poverty, indigenous rights, emergency aid, ecological justice, gender equity, and other fundamentally humanist goals who form nonstate networks and interest groups across national boundaries. From Greenpeace to Doctors Without Borders, from the Narmada Bachao Andolan to the Public Eye on Davos, the variety of these movements is vast, and their numbers seem to be growing all the time.

Social scientists have begun to notice that there is a complex convergence between what used to be seen in isolation as civil society institutions, transnational organizations, and popular social movements. In some loose way they can all be treated as NGOs or as transnational NGOs. But this is a huge category, ranging from churches and large philanthropic organizations to multilateral bodies and scientific societies. I am speaking here more narrowly of what Keck and Sikkink have called transnational activist networks (1997).

Such networks now are active in virtually every area of human equity and welfare ranging from health and environment to human rights, housing, gender, and indigenous people's rights. They are sometimes relatively local and regional in scope and sometimes truly global in their reach and impact. At the upper ends they are vast, well-funded, and widely known networks that have become mega-organizations. At the other end, they are small and fluid, bare networks, working quietly, often invisibly but also across national and other lines. The study of these networks has grown increasingly lively, especially among political scientists concerned with new forms of international bargaining, with expanding the study of social movements, and with the third space outside of market and state.

Many of these transnational activist networks are explicitly involved in the major debates about globalization, and some of them were made highly visible in the loudly publicized street protests of Seattle, Milan, Prague, Washington, D.C., Davos, and elsewhere in Europe and the United States in recent years. But the vast majority of these movements are engaged in much less publicized and much more targeted forms of advocacy and coordination in pursuit of specific policy changes at the local, national, and global levels. They have often succeeded in slowing down major official moves to set global policies on trade, environment, debt, and the like, usually by forcing transparency, by putting pressure on specific states, and by circulating information about forthcoming policy decisions rapidly across state boundaries by electronic means so as to mobilize protest.

Yet protest is not the key word with many of these movements, who also frequently explore partnerships with multilateral agencies, with their own home states, with major global funders, and with other forces in local and international civil society. These partnerships have not been explored very much by social scientists, and they constitute a crucial part of the David and Goliath leverage through which such networks have become effective.

I myself am engaged in a long-term study of one such important movement, the Shack/Slumdwellers International (SDI) and especially of its Indian node, which is an alliance of three different activist bodies: Society for the Promotion of Area Resource Centres, an NGO; Mahila Milan, an organization of poor urban women, with roots in Mumbai and devoted principally to small-scale savings and housing issues; and the National Slum Dwellers Federation, a remarkable older organization of male slum dwellers active in more than thirty cities in India. This troika of organizations, itself an unusual formation, has been functioning as an Alliance in India since the mid-1980s and has been a key member of SDI for about a decade. SDI is active in about twenty countries in Asia and Africa and has already made some major dents on such issues as establishing methods for leveraging people's savings movements to obtain bridge finance from major funders for pro-poor projects; in setting standards through which secure tenure in land and housing can be obtained for urban shack and pavement dwellers; and in contributing to the worldwide movement, notably led by countries like China, in making access to sanitary facilities a central goal of state policy. In working on these goals, what SDI (Appadurai 2000b) has done is to find new ways of organizing poor people in cities in the practices of what I have elsewhere called "deep democracy" (2002), in order to move away from existing models of agitational politics, or of simple downstreaming of charitable funds, or of simple outsourcing of traditional state functions, all paths that continue to be followed by many NGOs. Rather, SDI has focused on building the capacity of poor people in cities to explore and practice specific means of urban governance with an eye to building their own capacity to set goals, achieve expertise, share knowledge, and generate commitment. In this, they have made remarkable uses of such practices as daily savings, not to establish an entrepreneurial habit for the purpose of turning the urban poor into microcapitalists, but to establish certain protocols and principles for genuine self-governance. In effect, the urban poor that the Alliance has been able to "federate," their own key political term, have developed elements of a shadow urban government in many cities, notably in Mumbai, where they have established their own credible facilities to provide themselves with basic infrastructure and also with basic access to legal and political security.

What is most interesting about this exercise in capacity building (also organized through transnational exchanges between federations across countries for more than a decade) is that it has involved exploring and building new partnerships with members of local, state, and central governments in India, South Africa, Thailand, and Cambodia and more recently in Nepal, Zimbabwe, Kenya, and elsewhere. Ways have also been found to establish grounds for partnership with the United Nations system, notably with the United Nations Centre for Human Settlements, and even with the World Bank and other major state or quasi-state development bureaucracies in Europe, Africa, and Asia.

In this process, the Alliance has made remarkable strides in the substantial problems of urban poverty in many cities in India and beyond. Their global links, networks, exchanges, and perspectives have been key assets for them in strengthening the work and morale of their local federations. They have not only scaled up their ability to make material inter- ventions, for example, in the matter of relocating slum dwellers, building toilets, and creating savings-based housing cooperatives among the urban poor in many cities. They have also found new ways to channel these global exercises into building the capabilities of the poorest of the urban poor to be direct architects of their local political worlds. And, so far, amazingly, they have done so without becoming mere tools of state organizations, multilateral funders, political parties, or other major vested interests. This is cellular democratization at work.

The case of SDI and of other transnational housing movements, is of course, not unique. There are many such cellular formations in action, some more highly developed than others. Some are more visible, since they are involved in dramatic global issues such as the future of large dams. Others, working on humbler issues like housing and savings, are less visible. But they are all commonly involved in shaping a third space, in which markets and states are not only forced to recognize their importance but are in the process of having to concede genuine political space to these voices and actors when global decisions about key issues are made.

This is a not a fairy tale, nor is it at an end. It is a major struggle, filled with risks, hazards, contradictions, disappointments, and obstacles. But such movements are, in their aspirations, democratic both in form and in telos. And increasingly they are constructing the global not through the general language of universal problems, rights, or norms but by tackling one issue, one alliance, one victory at a time. The great progressive movements of the past few centuries, notably the working class movements which have characterized the nineteenth and twentieth centuries, always worked with universalist principles of solidarity, identity, and interest, for aims and against opponents, also conceived in universalist and generic terms. The new transnational activisms have more room for building solidarity from smaller convergences of interest, and though they may also invoke big categories, such as "the urban poor," to build their politics, they build their actual solidarities in a more ad hoc, inductive, and context-sensitive manner. They are thus developing a new dynamic in which global networking is put at the service of local imaginings of power.

Much else could be said about these movements, their form, function, and significance. But I need to return to the key themes of this essay. I point to such transnational and transurban activist movements because in their transnational character, they too work through the cellular principle, coordinating without massive centralization, reproducing without a clear-cut central mandate, working occasionally in the larger public eye but often outside it, leveraging resources from state and market to their own ends, and pursuing visions of equity and access that do not fit many twentieth-century models either of development or of democracy. We need to watch them, for the coming crisis of the nation-state may lie not in the dark cellularities of terror but in the utopian cellularities of these other new transnational organizational forms. Here lies a vital resource that could counter the worldwide trend to ethnocide and ideocide and here too lies the answer, however incipient, obscure, and tentative, to the strained relationship between peace and equity in the world we inhabit. At any rate, let us hope that this utopian form of cellularity will be the theater of our struggles. Otherwise, let us say goodbye both to civilians and to civility.

Bibliography

Anderson, Benedict R. 1991. *Imagined Communities: Reflections on the Origin and Spread of Nationalism*. London: Verso.

Appadurai, Arjun. 1996. *Modernity at Large: Cultural Dimensions of Globalization*. Minneapolis: University of Minnesota Press.

———. 1998a. "Full Attachment." *Public Culture* 10 (2).

———. 1998b. "Dead Certainty: Ethnic Violence in the Era of Globalization." *Public Culture* 10 (2): 225–47.

———. 2000a. "The Grounds of the Nation-State: Identity, Violence and Territory." In *Nationalism and Internationalism in the Post-Cold War Era*. Ed. Kjell Goldmann, Ulf Hannerz, and Charles Westin. London: Routledge.

———. 2000b. "Spectral Housing and Urban Cleansing: Notes on Millennial Mumbai." *Public Culture* 12 (3): 627–51.

———. 2002. "Deep Democracy: Urban Governmentality and the Horizon of Politics." *Public Culture* 14 (1): 21–47.

Arendt, Hannah. 1963. *Eichmann in Jerusalem: A Report on the Banality of Evil*. New York: Viking Press.

———. 1968. *The Origins of Totalitarianism*. New York: Harcourt.

Axel, Brian Keith. 2001. *The Nation's Tortured Body: Violence, Representation, and the Formation of a Sikh "Diaspora."* Durham and London: Duke University Press.

Balibar, Etienne. 1990. "The Nation Form." *Review* 12 (3): 329–61.

Basrur, Rajesh. M., ed. 2001. *Security in the New Millennium: Views from South Asia*. New Delhi: India Research Press.

Basu, Amrita. 1994. "When Local Riots Are Not Merely Local: Bringing the State Back In, Bijnor 1988–92." *Economic and Political Weekly*, 2605–21.

Bell, Daniel. 1961. *End of Ideology: On the Exhaustion of Political Ideas in the Fifties*. New York: Collier Books.

Castells, Manuel. 1996. *The Rise of the Network Society*. Cambridge: Blackwell.

Cooley, Charles Horton. 1964. *Human Nature and the Social Order*. Introduction by Philip Rieff. Foreword by Herbert Mead. New York: Schocken Books.

Das, Veena. 1990. *Mirrors of Violence: Communities, Riots and Survivors in South Asia*. Delhi: Oxford University Press.

Devji, Faisal. 2005. *Landscapes of the Jihad: Militancy, Morality and Modernity*. Ithaca: Cornell University Press.

Douglas, Mary. 1966. *Purity and Danger: An Analysis of Concepts of Purity and Taboo*. London: Routledge and Kegan Paul.

Friedman, Thomas. 1999. "A Manifesto for the Fast World." *New York Times*, March 28, 1999.

Fukuyama, Francis. 1992. *The End of History and the Last Man*. New York: Free Press.

Girard, René. 1977. *Violence and the Sacred*. Baltimore: Johns Hopkins University Press.

Goldhagen, Daniel. 1996. *Hitler's Willing Executioners: Ordinary Germans and the Holocaust*. New York: Knopf.

Goldmann, Kjell, Ulf Hannerz, and Charles Westin, eds. 2000. *Nationalism and Internationalism in the Post–Cold War Era*. London: Routledge.

Gourevitch, Philip. 1998. *We Wish to Inform You That Tomorrow We Will Be Killed with Our Families: Stories from Rwanda*. New York: Farrar, Straus and Giroux.

Hinton, Alexander Laban, ed. *Annihilating Difference: The Anthropology of Genocide*. Berkeley: University of California Press.

Huntington, Samuel. 1993. "The Clash of Civilizations." *Foreign Affairs* 72 (3).

———. 2004 "The Hispanic Challenge." *Foreign Policy*. March/April.

Ignatieff, Michael. 1998. *The Warriors Honor: Ethnic War and the Modern Conscience*. New York: Henry Holt.

Jaffrelot, Christophe. 2003. *India's Silent Revolution: The Rise of the Lower Castes in North India*. New York: Columbia University Press.

Jeganathan, Pradeep. 1997. "After a Riot: Anthropological Locations of Violence in an Urban Sri Lankan Community." PhD thesis, Department of Anthropology, University of Chicago.

———. 1998. "eelam.com: Place, Nation, and Imagi-Nation in Cyberspace." *Public Culture* 10 (3).

Kaviraj, Sudipta. 1992. "The Imaginary Institution of India." In *Subaltern Studies*, vol. 7. Ed. Partha Chatterjee and Gyanendra Pandey. Delhi: Oxford University Press.

Keck, Margaret E., and Kathryn Sikkink. 1997. *Activists Beyond Borders: Advocacy Networks in International Politics*. Ithaca: Cornell University Press.

Mbembe, Achille. 2003. "Necropolitics." *Public Culture* 15 (1): 11–40.

Merton, Robert King, and David L. Sills, eds. 2001. *Social Science Quotations: Who Said What, When, and Where*. New Brunswick, N.J.: Transaction Publishers.

Ortega y Gasset, José. 1957. *The Revolt of the Masses*. New York: Norton.

Patterson, Orlando. 1982. *Slavery and Social Death: A Comparative Study*. Cambridge, Mass.: Harvard University Press.

Scott, James C. 1998. *Seeing Like a State: How Certain Schemes to Improve the Human Condition Have Failed*. New Haven: Yale University Press.

Simmel, Georg. 1950. "The Stranger." In *The Sociology of Georg Simmel*. Trans. and ed. Kurt H. Wolff. Glencoe, Ill.: Free Press.

Uyangoda, Jayadeva. 2001. "Human Security, the State, and Democracy in a Globalising World." In *Security in the New Millennium: Views from South Asia*. Ed. Rajesh M. Basrur. New Delhi: India Research Press.

Weber, Eugene. 1976. *Peasants into Frenchmen: The Modernization of Rural France, 1880–1914*. Stanford: Stanford University Press.

Index

creation of minority groups, 41–46, 49–50, 84, 90–91, 112; state insecurity, 103–7; sum of uncertainty and incompleteness, 9–10, 84–85
crisis of circulation, 29–31
Croatia, x, 82

"Dead Certainty" (Appadurai), 5
deep democracy, 134–37. *See also* liberal democracy
Devji, Faisal, 85n1, 113n2
diasporic communities. *See* migration
discourse of terrorism, 15, 20
disjunctures of global flows, 29–31
Doctors Without Borders, 131
Douglas, Mary, 4, 44, 53

Eastern Europe, x, 82
economic contexts of globalization, 36–37; arms trafficking, 41; capitalist structures, 25–28; crisis of circulation, 29–31; high globalization, 2, 22–33, 129–31; migration of labor and capital, 37–40, 71, 83–84; poverty, xi; regulatory assurances of the nation-state, 25–26, 31; role of finance capital, 36; violence against minorities, 43. *See also* globalization

eelam.com, 24, 38
environmental issues, xi
ethnocidal violence, x, 1–10; anxiety of incompleteness and, 8–10; clash of ideocides and, 117–18; ideological certainty and, 90–92; intimate nature of, 127; the mask of the terrorist and, 89–90; nation-state contexts of cultural authenticity and, 23–25; as normative, 15–16; rage over minor differences and, 10–11, 82–85, 110; social uncertainty and, 5–9, 88–92; sum of uncertainty and incompleteness and, 9–10, 84–85; tipping points and, 58–59. *See also* predatory identities
ethnos, 3–4, 8, 22–23, 50–52; Indian majoritarian racism, 76–77; logic of ethnic purification, 91; Nazism, 52–59
European Union, 8, 63–64

fear of small numbers: in liberal democracies, 61–62; predatory rage and hatred and, 53, 58–59; special interest groups and, 62. *See also* minorities and marginalized groups; numbers
Fortuyn, Pim, 8
Freud's narcissism of minor differences, 11, 82–85, 110

146

immigration. *See* migration

India: Alliance of housing organizations in, 133–34; anti-Americanism in, 126; Babri Masjid attack in, x, 67, 94, 97; battle of conversions in, 70; caste and class politics in, 73–75; cellular democratization in, 133–37; condition of sufficiency in, 10; economic issues in, 27, 39; electoral vote bank in, 75–76, 111–12; elite migrations to the United States from, 123–25; ethnic uncertainty in, 5–9; Gujarat state in, 95, 110–11, 112; Hindu identity and power in, 66–77, 93–95, 104–6, 110–11, 126; human rights controversies in, 71–74; internal terrorism in, 93, 105–7; Kashmir struggles in, 93, 105, 106; kidnappings in, 12–13; *maha-arati* performances in, 98, 113n1; Mandal Commission in, 73–74; media roles in, 101–2; naval activity of, 98–99; nuclear weapons in, 105; Partition of, 66, 112; secularism in, 63–64, 72–73, 93; September 11, 2001 attacks and, 92–107; Shah Bano controversy in, 71–73; Shiva Sena party in, 98–99; Sikh-related violence in, 46; state insecurity in, 104–6; stereotypes of Muslims in, 70–72, 76–77; Uniform Civil Code (UCC) in, 72–73; violence against Muslims in, x, 8, 67, 69–77, 95, 105–6, 112; war on terror and, 20, 93. *See also* Mumbai; Muslims in India

Indian People's Party (BJP), 67; in elections of 2004, 68, 75–76, 95; in Gujarat, 95, 110–11, 112; Hindu Right agenda and, 93–95, 104–6; interest of, in war with Pakistan, 94; state insecurity and, 104–6

information technology, 27, 36–37, 129

insecurity of states, 103–9, 114n3

International Monetary Fund (IMF), 121, 126

Internet technology, 2; cellular nature of, 27–28; cyber communities and, 24–25; news and opinion flow and, 102

Iran-Iraq War, 118

Iraq: civil society building in, 81; ethnic dry-cleaning in, 82; long-distance democracy building in, 79–82; minority groups in, 80–81; potential for Islamic polity in, 80; U.S. invasion of, 20, 80–81, 92–93, 108; war with Iran, 118

Irish Republican Army, 130

tests of, against globalization, 132
Treaty of Westphalia, 26

uncertainty. *See* social uncertainty
United Nations: human rights conventions of, 64–65; international grassroots partnerships and, 135; vertebrate structure and, 25
United Nations Centre for Human Settlements, 135
United States: ambivalent multiculturalism of, 63–64; anti-Americanism and, 12–13, 102, 116, 118–31; Central Intelligence Agency, 126; Constitutional centrality of minority dissent in, 63–65; domestic violence in, 38–39; hatred of Islam in, 128; long-distance democracy building and, 79–82; minority rights in, 108; Oklahoma City bombing in, 108; prison industry in, 37–38; production of global inequality by, 23–24; reaction of, to September 11 attacks, 18–21, 107–9; special interest groups in, 62; use of military violence by, 102–3; war on terror of, 11–13, 20–21, 87–88; as world's police officer, 103.

See also September 11, 2001, terrorist attacks; war on terror
Uyangoda, Jayadeva, 114n3

vertebrate structures, 21, 25–31, 87, 100–101; geographic civilizations and, 115–16; in globalized contexts, 129–31. *See also* nation-states
victims of violence, 12–13
vivisectionist violence. *See* bodily violence

153

war on terror, 11–13, 92–93, 107–9; Afghanistan war and, 19–21, 79, 92–93, 108; Iraq war and insurgency and, 20, 80–81, 92–93, 108; naming the enemy in, 19, 20; as response to September 11 attacks, 18–21, 87–88, 107–9; vertebrate *vs.* cellular systems and, 21, 25–31
Weber, Max, 5, 40
Winfrey, Oprah, 120
World Bank, 121, 125, 126
World Trade Center attack of 1993, 108
World Trade Center attacks of September 11, 2001. *See* September 11, 2001, terrorist attacks

Yugoslavia, x, 82

Arjun Appadurai is the John Dewey Professor in the Social Sciences at the New School, where he is also Senior Advisor for Global Initiatives. His books include *Modernity at Large: Cultural Dimensions of Globalization* and the collection *Globalization*, also published by Duke University Press. He is a cofounder of the journal *Public Culture*; founder of the nonprofit PUKAR (Partners for Urban Knowledge, Action, and Research) in Mumbai; cofounder and codirector of ING (Interdisciplinary Network on Globalization); and a fellow of the American Academy of Arts and Sciences. He has served as a consultant or advisor to a wide range of public and private organizations, including the Ford, Rockefeller, and MacArthur foundations; UNESCO; the World Bank; and the National Science Foundation.

Library of Congress Cataloging-in-Publication Data

Appadurai, Arjun, 1949–
Fear of small numbers : an essay on the geography of
anger / Arjun Appadurai.
p. cm. — (Public planet books)
"A John Hope Franklin Center book."
Includes bibliographical references and index.
ISBN 0-8223-3834-3 (cloth : alk. paper)
ISBN 0-8223-3863-7 (pbk. : alk. paper)
1. Ethnic conflict. 2. Culture conflict.
3. Globalization—Social aspects. I. Title. II. Series.
HM1121.A67 2006
305.8009′049—dc22   2005037849